THE PREMIER GUIDE TO
Isle of

CW01072601

Editor & Principal Writer
Andrew Douglas
Managing Editor
Miles Cowsill
Contributors
Stan Basnett
Photography
Miles Cowsill
Published by
Lily Publications
Front Cover: Laxey Wheel
Back cover: Cregneash

All accommodation participates in the Isle of Man Department of Tourism and Leisure's grading scheme. If readers have any concern about the standards of any accommodation, please take the matter up directly with the provider of the accommodation, as soon as possible. Failing satisfaction, please contact the Isle of Man Department of Tourism and Leisure, Grading Department, The Sea Terminal, Peveril Square, Douglas, Isle of Man, IM1 2RG. Published by Lily Publications, 12 Millfields Close, Pentlepoir, Kilgetty, Pembrokeshire, Wales, SA68 0SA. Tel: (01834) 811895. Fax: (01834) 814484. ISBN 0 9517868 9 X

Contents

Welcome

The Isle of Man has the oldest continuous Parliament in the World and I am proud as a member of Tynwald, the Island's Parliament, to be able to play my part in passing on our tourism message by extending an invitation to you to visit our Island.

On the Island you will find a variety of traditions, ranging from our 1,000 year old Parliament, first set up by our Viking forefathers; steam trains that will shortly be celebrating their 125th year of operation, 100 year old electric tramcars, and horse drawn trams that have carried generations of holidaymakers up and down Douglas Promenade. There is also culture and attractions aplenty, including "The Story of Mann", a journey around the Island uniquely showing off our heritage in a truly international award winning manner.

Often described as "The Jewel in the Irish Sea", the Island is a veritable treasure chest of scenery with mountains, valleys, glens, cliffs, beaches, castles and beautiful rolling countryside forming a living collage. Add to that mixture a list of events and attractions and it easy to see why the tastes of most holidaymakers can be catered for. Equally important to us is the traditional warm Manx welcome offered to our visiting guests and to help you enjoy your visit still further I can recommend this well produced Guide Book. Lily Publications (IOM) have an established reputation for providing tourist information in a very readable form; this, the 1996/97 Guide book is no exception.

I do hope you can find time to visit us, I know you will enjoy the Isle of Man just as much as we will enjoy your company.

Hon Tony Brown MHK
Minister
Isle of Man Department of Tourism
and Leisure

The Premier Guide to a Premier Holiday Destination

Lily Publications' first guide to the Isle of Man appeared in 1994 and its immediate success led to Lily being short listed for consideration by the Isle of Man Department of Tourism and Leisure for the preparation of their official holiday brochure. Lily Publications were subsequently awarded the contract for the production of the Isle of Man Holiday Brochure for 1995, 1996 and 1997 and this Premier Guide to the Isle of Man sits very comfortably with that brochure giving the prospective visitor to the Island a more detailed picture of all that this beautiful Island has to offer.

Castletown

The Isle of Man is a separate and distinct nation, full of surprises for the first time or even the regular visitor to its shores. There are no counties for example, the Island is instead divided into Sheadings! No Members of Parliament, instead the members form Tynwald, the Island's own Government and are known as Members of the House of Keys or Members of the Legislative Council. Within the pages of this useful publication the Island is shown in its historical and political glory with continuous reference to the important heritage that marks it out as being so different from the rest of the British Isles.

Interested! This second and updated edition is presented in a brand new format giving a comprehensive guide to the history of the Island, beaches, coasts, towns, villages, mountains, valleys, glens, parks, days out by car and walks, along with a myriad of useful information on what to do and where to eat and a hundred and one activities to suit the individual, family or visiting special interest groups.

In this edition of The Premier Guide to the Isle of Man you have all you need to know to enjoy the pleasures and beauties of the Best of the British Isles.

Miles Cowsill
Managing Director
Lily Publications (IOM) Ltd

If peace & tranquillity are what you are looking for, where you can do as much or as little as you like, then The Isle of Man's Premier & only Four Star Hotel is the place to stay.

Our Wonderful Facilities include:

- 18 Hole Championship Length Golf Course
- Award winning Murray's Restaurant
- State of The Art Leisure Complex
- Crown Green Bowling
- Indoor Heated Swimming Pool
- Relaxing Bistro overlooking the 18th Hole
- Floodlit Driving Range & Tennis Courts
- And So Much More

Our Best Qualities are:

- A Home From Home Atmosphere, Far From The Madding Crowd
- At Affordable Prices, Isn't It Time You Had the Mount Murray Experience?

 HIGHLY COMMENDED

AA
★★★★

MOUNT MURRAY
HOTEL & COUNTRY CLUB
Santon, Isle of Man
Telephone: 01624 661111 • Facsimile: 01624 611116

RAC
★★★★

5

The Isle of Man
Britain's Treasured Island

S ince time immemorial the Isle of Man has offered to its visitors a glimpse of all that was good in the past, blended with a sense of anticipation of what the future might hold. Small in area, it has always managed to portray its beauty and delights, spreading the message in a manner that has reached every corner of the globe.

Geographically the Isle of Man lies midway between the coasts of England, Ireland, Scotland and Wales – "the adjacent islands". The Island measures at its extremities 33 miles (52kms) by 13 miles (22kms) and has a land mass area of some 227 square miles (572 sq.kms). It offers a wide variety of scenery covering virtually every type found elsewhere in the British Isles, ranging from vast stretches of open moorland, thickly wooded glens, to palm fringed ponds. Encompassed within over 100 miles (160kms) of coastline there is a central range of mountains and hills lying in a North Easterly/South Westerly direction with well defined valleys leading down to rocky cliffs and sheltered bays. This contrasts with the flat Northern plain's lazy rivers and streams meandering down to its long sandy beaches.

The Isle of Man has an equable climate lacking in extremes by virtue of its location and enjoying the warming influence of the Gulf Stream which flows around the shoreline. Prevailing winds blow from the South West, giving varying degrees of shelter and exposure island-wide due to the rugged nature of the topography. With the end of winter the improving weather of March and April is proving increasingly attractive to visitors. In summer, the months of May and June are usually the driest, whilst May, June and July are the sunniest. July and August are the warmest and more often than not, September and October enjoy fine weather.

Horse Riding

In recent years, there has been a growth in the resident population to the present level of some 70,000. This gives a density of just 308 people per square mile (122 per sq.km) and with about 40% of the Island being uninhabited, there is always plenty of room to move around. The major centre of population is based in Douglas, the capital, with approximately 22,000 residents, a further 28,000 live in seven other main towns and villages.

Contained within this green, pleasant and very fertile land are many surprises! The Island has the oldest continuous Parliament in the world, its own currency, stamps, telecommunications, language, castles, legends and customs, and they all come together with lots more to make the Isle of Man… "Britain's Treasured Island". Come on over and see for yourself.

TRAVEL BACK IN TIME

Discover the Isle of Man with Isle of Man Transport. The Victorian Manx Electric Railway, Snaefell Mountain Railway and Steam Railway offer a unique way to enjoy the Island in a relaxed and leisurely fashion.

The Isle of Man also has a well integrated bus network making just about every part of the island accessible.

So, from the top of Snaefell to Calf Sound, let Isle of Man Transport chauffeur you around our Island.

Special Island Freedom tickets offer a variety of ways to enjoy the Island's natural beauty, villages, towns and a wealth of visitor attractions.

RAMSEY

SNAEFELL

PEEL

DOUGLAS

CALF SOUND

Isle of Man transport

Strathallan Crescent
Douglas, Isle of Man IM2 4NR

TRAIN & BUS ENQUIRIES 01624 662525

FAILT ERRIU
ELLAN VANNIN – YN ELLAN SHIANT – ROIE-RAA

Neayr's traa erskyn towse, ta Mannin er jebbal da goaldee shilley jeh dy chooilley red va mie ayns ny shenn laghyn, kianlt seose marish roie-ennaghtyn jeh'n traa ry-heet. Ga dy vel ee beg, v'eh rieau cheet lhee dy hoilshaghey magh yn aalid as eunys eck, skeayley magh yn chaghteraght shen dy roshtyn gagh ard jeh'n chruinney.

Ta Ellan Vannin sy vean, eddyr Sostyn, Nerin, Nalbin as Bretin – 'ny hellanyn sniessey'. Ta lhiurid smoo yn Ellan 33 meeiley (52 km) as ta'n lheead smoo 13 meeiley (22 km), as she 227 meeiley kerrinagh (572 km kerr.) yn eaghtyr-thallooin jee. Shimmey reayrt-cheerey ta ry-akin ayns Mannin, goaill stiagh bunnys gagh sorch dy reayrt ta ry-akin ayns Ellanyn Sheear ny hOarpey, goll veih reeastaneyn mooarey gys glionteenyn lesh ymmodee biljyn gys puill chemmit lesh biljyn-palm. Cheu-sthie jeh 100 meeiley (160 km) as ny smoo jeh slyst-marrey, ta dreeym meanagh dy 'leityn as crink ta goll veih'n Chiar-hwoaie gys yn Cheear-ass lesh coanyn coon ta goll sheese dys eayninyn creggagh as baieaghyn fasteeagh. S'mooar yn anchaslys eddyr shen as awinyn as strooanyn litcheragh y thalloo rea twoaie ta goll dy moal dys ny traieyn geinnee liauyrey ayns shen.

Ta emshyr Vannin kenjal dy liooar kyndagh rish y voayl t'ee ayn, as ee goaill soylley jeh chiow y 'Trooan Gulf, ta goll mygeayrt-y-mooee. Ta'n thalloo sleitagh cur fastee ny lhiggey y raad da'n gheay neear-ass, y gheay chliaghtagh. Ta ny turryssee cheet dy choontey ny smoo jeh'n emshyr ayns Mee Vayrnt as Averil, ta sharaghey lurg y geurey. Sy tourey, ta Mee Boaldyn as Mean-souree cliaghtey ve ny meeghyn smoo chirrym, as ta'n emshyr smoo grianagh ayns Mee Boaldyn, Mean-souree as Jerrey-souree. She Jerrey-souree as Luanistyn ny meeghyn s'choe, as, son y chooid smoo, ta emshyr vraew ry-gheddyn ayns Mean-fouyir as Jerrey-fouyir.

Er y gherrid, ta earroo cummaltee Vannin er nirree gys red goll rish 70,000. Ta shen dy ghra, cha nel agh 308 persoonyn ayns gagh meeiley kerrinagh (122 ayns gagh km kerr.). Cha nel sleih cummal ayns 40% jeh'n Ellan, as myr shen ta kinjagh rheamys dy liooar dy gholl mygeayrt ayn. Ta'n chooid smoo jeh ny cummaltee ayns Doolish, yn ard-valley, lesh red goll rish 22,000 cummaltee. Cheu-mooie jeh shen, ta 28,000 dy 'leih cummal ayns shiaght baljyn elley.

Shimmey yindys t'ayns y cheer shoh, ta glass, taitnyssagh as feer hroaragh! Yn ard-whaiyl shinney sy teihll va chaglym gyn scuirr, as ny reddyn elley shoh s'lesh yn Ellan neesht: yn argid eck hene, ny cowraghyn-postagh, chellinsh, y chengey, cashtallyn, skeealyn as cliaghtaghyn. T'ad oilley cheet ry-cheilley lesh ram reddyn elley dy yannoo 'Yn Ellan Shiant' ass Mannin. Tar harrish as fow magh dhyt hene

PRÉSENTATION DE L'ÎLE DE MAN, JOYAU DES ÎLES BRITANNIQUES.
BIENVENUE À TOUS!

Depuis la nuit des temps, visiter l'île de Man c'est découvrir un peu ce qu'il y a eu de bon dans le passé tout en ayant un avant-goût de l'avenir. En dépit de sa petite taille, l'île a su témoigner de sa beauté et de ses merveilles aux quatre coins du monde.

Géographiquement, l'île de Man se trouve à mi-chemin entre les côtes anglaises, irlandaises, écossaises et galloises: les îles environnantes. L'île mesure à ses extrémités 52km sur 22km pour une superficie de 572km_. Elle présente une grande variété de paysages couvrant pratiquement tous ceux que l'on trouve dans les îles Britanniques: de grandes étendues de landes sauvages, des gorges couvertes de forêts denses, des étangs bordés de palmiers. Ceinturée de plus de 160km de côtes, la chaîne centrale de montagnes et de collines, orientée du nord-est au sud-ouest, possède de magnifiques vallées encaissées aboutissant à des falaises rocheuses et des baies abritées. Quel contraste saisissant avec la plaine uniforme du nord où les méandres des rivières et des cours d'eau aboutissent à de grandes plages sablonneuses!

L'île de Man jouit d'un bon climat, sans températures extrêmes, grâce à sa position et à l'influence du Gulf Stream qui réchauffe son littoral. Les vents soufflent principalement du sud-ouest et la nature escarpée du relief donne à cette île de grands contrastes avec des endroits exposés et d'autres abrités. Dès la fin de l'hiver, les visiteurs apprécient déjà l'amélioration progressive du temps au mois de mars et d'avril. En été, les mois de mai et de juin sont généralement les plus secs et mai, juin, juillet les plus ensoleillés. Juillet et août sont les plus doux et très souvent il fait encore beau en septembre et octobre.

Ces dernières années, la population a augmenté pour atteindre actuellement environ 70 000 habitants. Ceci représente une densité de 122 habitants au km_ et comme 40% de l'île est inhabitée, il y a encore beaucoup de place. Une grande partie de la population est concentrée dans la capitale, Douglas, qui compte environ 22 000 habitants, les sept autres villes et villages principaux regroupent 28 000 personnes.

Ce pays verdoyant, plein de charme et extrêmement fertile réserve bien des surprises! L'île a le plus ancien parlement du monde en exercice sans interruption, sa propre monnaie, timbres, télécommunications, langue, châteaux, légendes et coutumes. Il y aurait bien plus à dire sur l'île de Man, le joyau des îles Britanniques, alors il vaut mieux y aller soi-même pour découvrir ses merveilles.

Maughold Head

WELKOM
HET EILAND MAN – ENGELAND'S BEST BEWAARDE EILAND – EEN INLEIDING

Sinds onheuglijke tijden heeft het eiland Man zijn bezoekers een vluchtige blik geboden op alles wat goed was in het verleden, vermengd met een voorgevoel van wat de toekomst zou kunnen brengen. Klein in oppervlakte, is het altijd in staat geweest zijn schoonheid en genoegens op zodanige wijze af te schilderen, dat de boodschap over de gehele aarde is verspreid.

Geografisch gezien ligt het eiland Man in het midden tussen de kusten van Engeland, Ierland, Schotland en Wales – "de aangrenzende eilanden". Het eiland meet tussen de uiteinden 33 bij 13 mijl (52 bij 22 km.) en heeft een oppervlakte van ongeveer 227 vierkante mijl (572 vierkante km.). Het biedt een grote verscheidenheid aan natuurschoon met vrijwel elk type dat elders op de Britse Eilanden te vinden is, variërend van uitgestrekte heides en dik beboste bergdalen tot met palmen omzoomde plassen. Omringd door meer dan 100 mijl (160 km.) kustlijn ligt een centraal bergketen in een noordoost/zuidwestelijke richting met duidelijk begrensde valleien die naar steile rotsen en beschutte baaien aflopen. Dit vormt een kontrast met de trage rivieren en stromen die zich van de noordelijke vlakte naar de lange zandstranden aldaar omlaag slingeren.

Het eiland Man heeft een gelijkmatig klimaat zonder uitersten tengevolge van zijn positie binnen de verwarmende invloed van de Golfstroom die langs de kust stroomt. De heersende wind is zuidwestelijk en tengevolge van de ruwe topografie wordt men hier afwisselend tegen beschut en aan bloot gesteld. Het beter wordende weer tegen het einde van de winter in maart en april blijkt steeds aantrekkelijker te worden voor bezoekers. In de zomer zijn de maanden mei en juni gewoonlijk het droogst, terwijl mei, juni en juli het zonnigst zijn. Juli en augustus zijn het warmst en meestal is het in september en oktober mooi weer.

In de laatste jaren was er een groei in de vaste bevolking naar het huidige niveau van ongeveer 70.000. Dit geeft een bevolkingsdichtheid van net 308 personen per vierkante mijl (122 per vierkante km.) en daar ongeveer 40% van het eiland onbewoond is, is er altijd genoeg bewegingsruimte. Het belangrijkste bevolkingscentrum is Douglas, de hoofdstad, met circa 22.000 inwoners, terwijl er nog 28.000 wonen in zeven andere grotere steden en dorpen.

In dit groene, aangename en zeer vruchtbare land liggen veel verassingen! Het eiland heeft het oudste onafgebroken parlement ter wereld, zijn eigen muntstelsel, postzegels, telecommunicaties, taal, kastelen, legendes en douane, en dit alles samen met nog veel meer maken het eiland Man... "Engeland's best bewaarde eiland". Kom zelf maar kijken.

WILKOMMEN
DIE INSEL MAN – DIE BELIEBTE INSEL GROSS BRITANNIENS – WIR STELLEN VOR:

Seit Urzeiten bot die Insel Man ihren Besuchern einen flüchtigen Eindruck von allem, was in der Vergangenheit gut war – verbunden mit Erwartungen dafür, was die Zukunft bringen würde. Obgleich sie klein ist, hat sie es stets verstanden, ihre Schönheit und Köstlichkeiten in das rechte Licht zu rücken und sich in einer Weise mitzuteilen, daß sie jeden Winkel der Welt erreichte.

Geographisch liegt die Insel Man in der Mitte zwischen der englischen, irischen, schottischen und walisischen Küste – "den Nachbarinseln". Die Insel mißt an den äußersten Punkten 52 km mal 22 km und hat eine Landmasse von etwa 572 km². Sie bietet die verschiedensten Landschaftsbilder, wie sie an anderen Stellen auf den britischen Inseln zu finden sind, von offenen Hochmoorflächen, dicht bewaldeten Tälern bis zu mit Palmen umringten Teichen. Von über 160 km Küste umgeben, verläuft in nordöstlicher/südwestlicher Richtung in der Inselmitte ein Gebirgszug mit gut ausgebildeten Tälern, die in felsigen Klippen und geschützten Buchen enden. Dies steht im Kontrast zu den träge fließenden Bächen und Flüssen der flachen nördlichen Ebenen, die sich zu langen, sandigen Stränden schlängeln.

Auf der Insel Man herrscht ein ausgeglichenes Klima ohne Extreme, bedingt durch ihre Lage und den Einfluß des warmen Golfstromes, der ihre Küste umspielt. Der Wind weht meist aus Südwesten. Dabei ist die ganze Insel durch ihre zerklüftete Topographie unterschiedlich geschützt oder dem Wind ausgesetzt. Nach Ende des Winters erweist sich das bessere Wetter im März und April für Besucher immer attraktiver. Im Sommer sind die Monate Mai und Juni gewöhnlich am trockensten, während Mai, Juni und Juli am sonnigsten sind. Juli und August sind am wärmsten, und in den meisten Fällen herrscht im September und Oktober schönes Wetter.

In den letzten Jahren nahm die Bevölkerung auf den derzeitigen Stand von etwa 70.000 zu. Damit entsteht eine Bevölkerungsdichte von ganzen 257 Einwohnern pro Quadratkilometer, und da etwa 40% der Insel unbewohnt sind, bietet sie immer genug Bewegungsfreiheit. Douglas, die Hauptstadt, hat die meisten Einwohner, etwa 22.000. Weitere 28.000 wohnen in sieben anderen größeren Städten und Dörfern.

Das grüne, angenehme und sehr fruchtbare Land bietet viele Überraschungen! Die Insel kann sich des ältesten fortgesetzten Parlaments der Welt rühmen, einer eigenen Währung, eigenen Sprache, Briefmarken, eines eigenen Fernmeldewesens, Schlössern, Legenden und Gebräuchen, und durch alles zusammen und vieles andere wird die Insel Man zur "beliebten Insel Großbritanniens". Besuchen Sie uns. Überzeugen Sie sich selbst.

Birth of an Island

Despite the legend that the Isle of Man was hurled into the sea by the Irish giant Finn Mac Coole, we do know that something moved in those crystal waters in the far off days of pre-history.

Something was stirring at the bottom of the ocean. Over a period of millions of years the mud and sand became hardened into rock. Squeezed together by unimaginable forces these rocks found their way to the surface to begin their long progress into the mountains, hills, precipitous cliffs, valleys, glens and plains that we know today. At times the Isle of Man has been connected to the adjacent islands of England, Ireland, Wales and Scotland ... at other times not. Occasionally these hidden forces broke forth pouring lava and ash out onto the land, as can still be witnessed between Scarlett Point and Poyll Vaaish. Throughout time the sea has always remained pre-eminent in the Island's life and history.

Thousands of years ago, ancient Mann protruded above the ice in the shape of three islands, a form now scarcely recognisable, save for the high lands of the North, South and the Mull Peninsula. As the ice retreated the harsh landscape was sculptured into its present form. In its farewell, the ice left behind the gift of the lovely rolling Bride hills, formed from glacial deposits.

Pre-history

Now lying quietly in the Irish Sea, the Isle of Man has seen many changes in both physical and human terms as it emerged from its formation into the dawn of history itself. It now seems hardly credible as modern man gazes down into the central valley between Douglas and Peel, that this was once the seabed, or that as you drive between

New Stone Age burial site

Port St Mary and Port Erin this whole area was covered in water and ice. Who were the first settlers? The evidence points to Stone Age man, before he was overwhelmed by the physically larger Celts, as they were driven westwards by the all conquering Germans and Romans.

Settling into a very pleasant and fertile land suited the new immigrants who belonged to a separate and very distinct tribe from the Celts to the south and east. The Gaelic branch to which the Manx, Irish and Scots belong and the Cymric or Brythonic to which the Welsh and Bretons owe allegiance can still easily identify with each other by language although there are many cultural differences. It is probably towards the Irish that there developed the greatest similarities ... and so the Celtic people of Mann settled into a routine of common land owning, farming and generally living a peaceful existence totally undisturbed by the Romans and, save for an occasional marauding raid by passing Anglo-Saxons, remaining isolated from the outside world.

The coming of the Norsemen

This peaceful state of affairs could not last forever. By the end of the eighth century the Island was about to receive its first visitors. No ordinary tourists these ... they were the Vikings, who had by this time begun their wanderings in search of plunder around the British islands, western and southern Europe. The sea held no fear for these brave and warlike warriors who believed that plundering was an honourable occupation. The long sandy and sometimes gravelly beaches of the North and West of the Island proved more than suitable for their longboats to be run ashore and there was shelter aplenty to the South and East. Fifty years or so after their first arrival, they began to settle down to a life ashore and this is evident in the names of some of our farms, mountains, hills, villages and people to this very day. Many of the names may sound strange to the visitor, so where possible the translation into English is shown alongside the Manx, Norse, Scandinavian or Irish.

The Norse settlers in their language used *by* as the ending to many of their words and so you have

Kirby meaning Church farm, *Colby* meaning Kolli's farm, *Jurby* as Ivar's farm, and there are many other words of Scandinavian extract. For example *Snaefell* means Snow Mountain, *Sartfell* is Black Hill.

Sulby still exists as a village, in those far off days it was known as Solvi. On the lips of a Gaelic speaking people these new words took on a different pronunciation and so you have the Norse names such as *Ottarr* becoming Cottier, *Thorketill* as Corkhill, *Thorliotr* ending up as Corlett and so on. Gradually with the integration of the Norsemen into the Celtic way of life many of our commonest surnames began to emerge such as Brew, Bridson, Cain, Caley, Callister, Callow, Cannell, Cashen, Clucas, Curphey, Cowin, Kaighan, Kelly, Kewley, Mylchreest, Mylrea, Quayle, Quiggin and Quinney as well as many others.

With the coming together of the two races, the Island began a further period of turbulent development. Tradition tells of the arrival of the first Norse King of Man, *Goree* or Orry as we now know him, at the Lhane in Jurby who, when asked where he came from, responded by pointing at the Milky Way and said "that is the road to my country". The Manx thereafter knew the Milky Way as *Yn raad mooar Ree Goree*, "The great road of King Orry".

During the period the Isle of Man was under Viking control it was ruled at various times by kings who sometimes lived in Dublin, Northumbria or in Mann itself. After a short spell in the hands of the Norse rulers of Limerick towards the end of the tenth century, it became subject to the rule of the Earls of Orkney before falling under the domination of the Kings of Dublin once again. In 1079, Godred Crovan, son of Harald the Black of Iceland, came to conquer Mann. After being defeated by the Manx in his first two battles against them, he returned and in his third attack was successful, largely because he hid three hundred of his followers amongst the trees on Sky Hill above Milntown. Because he had been well received by the Manx on fleeing to the Isle of Man after the defeat of Harald, King of Norway, at the battle of Stamford Bridge in 1066, he spared the defeated Manx. Following the battle he contented

Herring Tower, Langness

A Manx Thatched Cottage

himself with dividing the Island in two, with the Manx retaining the northern half and the Vikings living in the southern half. Godred's descendants were to rule Mann for nearly two hundred years.

During the transition period from warriors of the seas to landowners and farmers, the Vikings left the Celts, who for a while were little more than slaves, to run the farms and harvest the crops. The Norsemen busied themselves trading with the adjacent islands, Iceland and the South of Europe. Probably their best known occupation on land was to carve beautiful crosses, many fine examples of which still exist today dotted about in our churchyards and museums.

Without doubt the greatest single gift the Vikings donated to the Isle of Man was the system of government which still exists today. The historian will tell you that Tynwalds or Things as the Vikings called them were probably held in each sheading. These smaller Things came together at least once a year under the auspices of a great Thing for the whole Island. After more than one thousand years of continuous parliamentary government, the Island still remains well placed in the forefront of democracy, and the modern Manx

Nation continues to export and trade its products to the rest of the world much as their Viking forefathers did many centuries ago.

Monks and Bishops

Although the Vikings eventually became Christians, it was not before they had extinguished the light of Christianity which had burned brightly on Mann from about the fourth century onwards. Around the beginning of the eleventh century the Manx began once again to embrace Christianity. Although written evidence is scanty, from the time of the founding of Rushen Abbey by the Cistercians of Furness Abbey in Barrow, it is possible to get a clearer picture of developments from the writings of the monks.

The Manx bishops are known as the Bishops of Sodor and Man, and the earliest reference to the Diocese of Sodor and Man seems to be in 1154. Consisting of the southern islands of Scotland, it extended from the Hebrides to Arran and the Isle of Man itself. Sodor owes its derivation to two Norse words meaning southern isles, so in fact Sodor and Man means "The southern Isles and Man".

Bishops have always played an important role in the history of this fair land, sometimes leading the people by good example, at other times abusing their power and privileged position. In 1266 the connection between the "Isles and Sodor" came to an end, although the diocese continued to be under the rule of a distant Norwegian Archbishop until the fifteenth century. It was during this period the Island had been divided into parishes.

After Norse rule had come to an end, the Isle of Man was the subject of many struggles which saw its ownership passing between the Scots and the English. It was not until 1346 that the Island came firmly and finally under English rule. During this period immediately before the long reign of the Stanleys, the Island's people suffered grievously. Contemporary writings of the time report that the Island was "desolate and full of wretchedness". In another report the writer told of a great battle on the slopes of South Barrule in which the Manx were heavily defeated by Irish freebooters who plundered everything of value. Only the purchase of corn from Ireland saved the people from starvation. So poor were the Islanders

that they could no longer afford to make any more of the magnificent crosses for which they had been renowned in earlier times.

The Stanleys

The Stanley dynasty which was to rule the Isle of Man from 1405 – 1736 presented their first King of Man as Sir John Stanley I. He never came to the Island and was succeeded by his son Sir John Stanley II a wise but somewhat despotic ruler, who at least conferred some benefits on the people. It is recorded that there were two revolts against his authority. To prevent a repetition he increased the power of the governors, and at this period he substituted trial by battle with trial by jury as a means of settling disputes. Many of his successors did not visit this, their kingdom, and those who did come, often only paid a fleeting visit.

History records that we had to wait for James Stanley, the 7th Earl of Derby, for the next major turning point in the story of Mann. In 1643 James, or as the Manx people called him, *Yn Stanlagh Mooar*, The Great Stanley, was ordered by King

Castle Rushen

Charles I of England to go to the Isle of Man and put down a threatened revolt by the Manx. Hiding an iron hand in a velvet glove he soon made himself popular. Although the people of this period enjoyed peace never had they had less liberty. In fact they were actually deprived of their ancient tenure or, in other words, the right to hold land.

Illiam Dhone

With Charles II on the throne of England, *Yn Stanlagh Mooar* proved his loyalty once more to the Crown and threw in his lot with the Royalists. Leading his troops, three hundred Manxmen amongst them, he set off in support of the King. Disaster overtook those brave men and Stanley himself was executed. At this time the great Manx patriot William Christian, *Illiam Dhone* appeared ... to save the people from disaster.

Illiam Dhone, which translated into English means "Brown William", anticipated punitive action against the Islanders and gathered together the people at Ronaldsway to assess the future. Dispatching the militia to capture all military

installations he achieved total success, with the exception of Peel and Rushen castles, which were soon given up by Stanley's widow, and the Island eventually surrendered to the Parliamentarians.

William Christian paid a terrible price for his actions. After the Restoration and some ten years after leading the revolt against the Countess of Derby, *Illiam Dhone* was shot to death on Hango Hill at Castletown.

The Atholls, the Smuggling Trade, Decay and the British Crown

The 1700's were turbulent years for the Manx Nation. They saw the end of the Stanleys' rule, serious disputes with the English Parliament, and the destruction of the smuggling trade which was just about the only way the Island had been financially "kept afloat". On the credit side it saw the passing of The Act of Settlement in 1704, which is effectively the Island's Magna Carta, and in 1736 under the rule of the 2nd Duke of Atholl, the Manx Bill of Rights was introduced. This Bill in effect did away with despotic government and

Island Photographic

Tynwald Day

replaced it with oligarchical government or, in other words, the Keys, the lower house of Tynwald, once more reverted to self election. Constitutional Government was just around the corner.

Working hard for the people over half a century during this era was the much loved Bishop Thomas Wilson. Bishop of Sodor and Man for fifty eight years, he fed the populace in times of crop failure, promoted education, established schools and libraries around the Island, and laboured long on behalf of the Manx State.

On the 11th July 1765 the Island passed into the ownership of the British Crown. As the Manx standard was lowered at Castle Rushen and the Union flag raised, George III was proclaimed King of Man ... John the 3rd Duke of Atholl had sold the Island to the Imperial Parliament for £70,000. The prosperity of the Island, such as it was, disappeared overnight with the demise of the smuggling trade and London appeared well satisfied. This was not to be the end of the Atholl connections with the Isle of Man.

As the Island fell into decay and its people into despair, the Government in London felt obliged to try and rectify this parlous state of affairs and in 1793 appointed the 4th Duke of Atholl to be Governor. This appointment was not a success and in 1829 he severed his relationship with the Island for the sum of £417,000 and left. George IV, King of Great Britain and Ireland became Lord of Man. The period immediately after the Duke's departure saw little change. London continued to control the Island's revenue, and the House of Keys still largely ignored the peoples' wishes by electing one of their "own" whenever a vacancy in the House occurred. Help was at hand though in the form of Mr. Henry Loch, later to be Lord Loch and after whom part of Douglas Promenade is named.

Appointed as Governor in 1863, Henry Loch brought energy and a real sense of purpose to the position. Working closely with Tynwald Court, lengthy negotiations with Her Britannic Majesty's Government were eventually concluded in 1866 to ensure that after the running expenses of the Manx Government were met, any surpluses could be retained on the Isle of Man for improvements to a fledgling infrastructure. Part of the agreement called for the House of Keys to be popularly elected and for the English Government to receive a sum of £10,000 annually from insular revenue as a contribution towards the defence of the Realm, a payment that, although much increased, continues to this very day.

Early Tourism

Even before the arrival of Governor Loch, the Island had started to become popular as a tourist destination. Certainly with more and more of the revenue being retained locally and spent on improving the infrastructure, it was not too long before the population increased and communications to and from the Island vastly improved. Towards the end of the 1800's as the railways and their associated shipping companies opened up the adjacent islands to travel for all, tourism in the Isle of Man mushroomed. Much of the infrastructure that exists today owes its initial development to this period. Hotels, trains, piers, theatres, reservoirs, steamships and roads all played their part in thrusting the Island to the forefront of the domestic British leisure market.

As the new post Victorian era arrived, the Island rose to the challenge of mass tourism and for decades happily served the Lancashire cotton workers, the Yorkshire miners, Scottish engineers, Geordie ship builders and a whole host of other folk and their families as they sought their annual escape from a life of hard work to the fair shores of Ellan Vannin. A tradition that was only interrupted by two world wars.

During the twentieth century the Isle of Man, like many other places around the world, has witnessed change to its economy. As the old and traditional industries declined, new methods of sustaining the population arose; as our motto says, *Quocunque Jeceris Stabit ... Which Ever Way You Throw Me I Will Stand*. Investment in tourism continues apace. What has never changed though, is the traditional Manx welcome offered to our visitors. Please enjoy our Island as much as we enjoy your visiting us.

The ISLE
Britain's Trea

Isle·of
MAN

of MAN
sured Island

I t's a busy world and we all need to spend quality time to relax and recharge our batteries.

Visit the Isle of Man and you'll find one of the world's most beautiful Islands lying in the middle of the Irish sea, with a pace of life that is unique.

Take a walk and you'll discover natural beauty, breathtaking scenery and unspolit beaches, or take in the many leisure activities that the Island offers from first class golfing to sailing. The Isle of Man is steeped in heritage and is a treasure chest waiting to be discovered.

If you're thinking of taking that well deserved break you'll be pleasantly surprised at what the Isle of Man has to offer.

For further details, and to receive your free copy of the 1996 Holiday Guide, please telephone 0345 686868.

Alternatively you can write to Department of Tourism, Sea Terminal, Douglas, Isle of Man, IM1 2RG.

For such a small Island there is a wide variety of choice when it comes to a day out on the beach and there is always a sheltered one to find. If you are an expert on sandcastles the range runs from the good bonding sand of Port Erin and Douglas beaches to the fine sand of Peel and the difficult to work with, dune sands of the North West beaches. Most beaches are safe but that always depends on the responsible attitude adopted by beach users ... so please, always take care. There are many currents flowing around the Island's coastline and the dangerous waters of the Calf Sound and at the Point of Ayre bear witness to that fact, and at least they are visible as a turbulent line of water.

All beaches on the Isle of Man are owned by the Government up to the high water mark and there are no charges for their use. Some beaches are inaccessible, others are difficult to reach and with a mean tidal range of 24 feet it really does pay to keep an eye on the incoming tide. Where access to beaches is by means of the coastal footpath or across headlands, please remember the Isle of Man is very much a rural area and observe the code of the countryside. Due to the isolation of some of our beaches basic facilities may well be scarce but most of the major towns and villages are well served with shops, banks, toilet facilities etc..

Port Erin

East Coast

Cranstal to Maughold Head

On the East coast the sandy beaches commence at *Cranstal*, a Treen or Homestead once upon a time possibly belonging to someone called Kraun. Just a little further on is *Shellag Point*, Seal Creek or Bay, but any indentation of the shore disappeared long ago as a consequence of the continuous erosion of the coastline. Good fishing along this beach all the way into Ramsey.

Ramsey has plenty of relaxation to offer and while Mum and Dad enjoy a break the youngsters can enjoy a sail or a canoe trip on the Mooragh Lake. The public park here, close to Ramsey seafront, presents a number of amusements and is a favourite place for tourists. Excellent sandy beach from the South of the harbour entrance to *Port Lewaigue*, which means Creek. The other side of a headland known as *Gob ny Rona*, Point of the Seal, has a nice beach in the pretty little cove of *Port e Vullen*, a name the meaning of which is lost in the mists of time. This is the last sandy beach until Laxey.

Amenities:

21

Peaceful Beaches

Maughold to Laxey

Between Maughold Head, the Latin form of the Irish for *St Machud*, and Laxey there are a number of rocky coves such as the Dhoon, with stony beaches and whilst swimming is not recommended, they are a treat to visit with something on offer for all age groups. Laxey beach and harbour will keep you well occupied. There is always something going on and even doing nothing can be a pleasant experience. Many people hop on the tram to Laxey and entertain themselves quite easily. A walk up the Glen Road makes a change from beach life and the Village Commissioners' bowling green and tennis courts offer the opportunity of a little competitive exercise. The Laxey Glen Gardens are a pleasant spot to picnic in.

Amenities: 🚾 ✕ 🏛 ♨ 📞 🎣 *i*

Laxey to Douglas

Across the bay from Laxey is Garwick Bay. There is a very rocky shore here and without doubt it is best to leave your vehicle on the main road above the beach and walk. The access road is very steep and should only be attempted if you are fit. Next stop is Groudle Beach which is reached by taking the minor slip road just up the hill from the main glen entrance. Groudle is making great efforts to recapture some of its old glories and leading the way is the Groudle Railway Company celebrating its centenary in 1996. If your hobby is trains, the miniature railway winding its way round the North headland gives immense pleasure. Onchan has no beaches although it can lay claim to a couple of small inlets, one of which rejoices in the magnificent name of Onchan Harbour

Douglas can boast one of the finest sweeps of any bay in the British Isles. There are plenty of leisure activities in Douglas and if you need information on a wide range of sports and entertainment then the friendly staff at the Tourist Information Office, or the hotel reception will be only too pleased to guide and advise you. Starting to the South of Port Jack the rocky beach soon gives way to almost one and a half miles of sand, fringed with a border of shingle. It offers endless hours of pleasure to all generations and what better way to travel along the promenades than by horse drawn tram or "toasties" as the locals call them.

Amenities: ⓦ ✕ ⚏ ⛫ ☎ ☗ *i*

Douglas to Derbyhaven

Leaving the sands of Douglas behind, the coastline offers many coves and inlets all the way down to Derbyhaven, the largest of which is Port Soderick. Many are accessible by vehicle, some only on foot all offer something different. Derbyhaven is now very much a water leisure centre, although there is an area of sandy beach towards the hotel on the North side of the Langness peninsula. If you are a golfer then play the famous Castletown Golf Links course. The 17th hole on this course is every bit as exciting as the famous Turnberry lighthouse hole.

South Coast

Castletown to Port St Mary

Castletown beach although much smaller than Douglas has an imposing back drop, with the harbour, castle and town combining to give it a feeling of timelessness. The peace and quiet does get shattered on occasions such as in August when the World Tin Bath Championships are held in the harbour and again in September when the International Rally cars have a special stage passing through the town. During International Cycle Week a Kermess is held which is a very exciting spectacle as the cyclists race around the streets. To the South and West of the town the shoreline gives way to lava beds and rough, jagged, needle-like rocks and it is not until you reach the bottom of Fishers Hill, A7, that a small sandy beach is again encountered. The western end of *Bay ny Carrickey* offers plenty of space to indulge in all sorts of water-borne or shore-based activities and a short walk round Gansey Point bring you to Chapel Bay, a children's playground for centuries. If you are keen on yachting, there are plenty of boats to see in the beautiful inner and outer harbours of Port St Mary.

Amenities: ⓦ ✕ ⚏ ⛫ ☎ ☗ *i*

Port St Mary to Port Erin

The high cliffs of the Mull Peninsula between Port St Mary, The Sound and Port Erin prevent any kind of casual beach activity and they are best viewed from a boat or strictly left to the skilled rock climbers. During the summer months the local yachts provide entertainment as they dash about the bays. There are a number of well signposted footpaths covering the area but please remember cliff walking can be dangerous, especially in windy conditions. Port Erin beach is best described as a jewel in the crown. Golden sands, rocky inlets, a small cave or two, boats and even its own beach lighthouse; it has everything to offer the beach lover. Make the most of the sand here, as apart from one or two strands of beach, the rest of the accessible foreshores from Port Erin to Peel are rock, shingle and boulder strewn.

Amenities: ⓦ ✕ ⚏ ⛫ ☎ ☗ *i*

West Coast

Fleshwick to Peel

Fleshwick from the Scandinavian word *Flesvik* meaning green spot creek, must have been attractive to our seafaring forefathers as it affords excellent shelter from all but the most northerly of winds. The views looking North from Fleshwick are memorable and as you stand on the rocky beach, sense the atmosphere of past traditions all around this cliff edged creek. Niarbyl is a favourite beach for families offering ample opportunities to examine the rocks and explore tidal pools. Just to the South of Niarbyl below Cregganmoar farm is a beach with a small sandy shore at low water. It is a difficult walk for youngsters with access via the cliff top.

The fine sand at Peel is very difficult to use for sand castles when dry, so the experts advise. This should not put you off, far from it, just move a little closer to the water's edge, it is much more pliable. The beach at Peel is ideal for motorcycle sandraces and it really comes to life when the Go-cart Grand Prix is run around the narrow streets.

Amenities: ⊞ ✗ ♿ ⊟ ☎ ☕ *i*

Peel to Kirk Michael

From a little North of Peel it is possible with care and the right tidal conditions to embark on a beach walk which, if you have the energy, will bring you right along the water's edge to Ramsey. The first few miles are along gently sloping beaches bordered by eroding sandy cliff faces. High up above the A3, past the Devil's Elbow in the direction of Kirk Michael is *Ballacarnane* Farm, Homestead of the Cairn and home now to the Cannell family. The land here, if it could speak would tell tales of great incidents in the history of this small land, stories that would make the very hairs stand up on the back of your neck. The land cannot speak for itself, so nowadays the story telling is best left to those who know the area. The Cannell family of Ballacarnane have farmed there for centuries and Mr Cannell is the Captain of the Parish.

Glen Mooar, Great Glen, marks the old border between the parishes of Kirk Michael and Kirk German and is a mixture of sandy cliffs and smooth rocks giving access to miles of beach. A great place for seal watching! Kirk Michael has an easy approach to the beach via Glen Wyllin and is easily identified by the sandstone pillars of the former railway viaduct. Please take care in the vicinity of the cliffs and dunes, sand can move without warning.

Amenities: ⊞ ✗ ♿ ⊟ ☎ ☕ *i* ⚲

North Coast

Kirk Michael to Cranstal

Leaving Kirk Michael behind, the beaches run northwards with entry via a number of lanes leading off the main roads. Most of these lanes have car parks at the seaward end and are within a few yards of the shore. Ballaugh, Blue Point and Rue Point are all worthy of a visit and at low water the casual stroller in this area is sometimes rewarded with glimpses of old wrecks which met their end on what can sometimes be a wild and inhospitable coast.

The nearer you get to the Point of Ayre the more the rambler notices an almost subtle change from dune country to tightly knitted heather clad fields and then onto steeply shelving stone beaches, as you round the Point. Gradually the cliffs increase in height up to Cranstal and then you are back to eroding sandy cliffs and if you have walked the whole way from just North of Peel then you are on the "last legs" of a very demanding walk.

Safety on the Beach

* **Know where your children are at all times**. Keep an eye on them, especially when they are swimming or playing on the water's edge. Children can drown even in very shallow water.

* **Make sure you always know where everyone else is**. Let each other know if anyone is going swimming or leaving the beach for any reason.

* **Beware of being trapped by the tide coming in**. You can find out about local currents by asking the local Harbour Master or the Coastguard, especially if you are going to a remote beach.

* **Don't play on rocks**. Take care on groynes and breakwaters – they can be dangerous. Note where they are before you start swimming.

* **Never climb on cliffs and keep away from cliff edges**. Even gentle slopes can be dangerous when they are wet. Never tunnel in sand cliffs or dunes.

* **Watch out for large waves coming in**. They can sweep you off your feet even if you think you are standing somewhere safe.

* **Always obey any notices or instructions**.

Safety in the Water

NEVER SWIM:

- if you feel unwell.
- for at least an hour after a meal (you may get cramp).
- when you are cold or tired.
- if you have been drinking alcohol.

* Always swim where there are other people.

* Always swim close to the beach and don't swim out to sea.
* Don't stay in the water too long. You will get cold and tired.
* Don't use inflatable airbeds in the water. They can get blown out to sea.
* If you have a belly board, stay with the board and don't go out too far.
* Only use a snorkel if you are a good swimmer and the water is calm. Don't snorkel if you have breathing problems.

IF YOU SEE SOMEONE IN TROUBLE IN THE WATER

tell the Coastguard or police by dialling 999.

Tide Information

Tide times in the Isle of Man are based on high water Liverpool plus or minus the following differences:
Calf Sound + 0.05 mins Douglas – 0.04 mins
Peel – 0.02 mins Ramsey + 0 04 mins
Remember to add the hour for Summer Time. Tidal information can be obtained from the local press or from Manx Radio immediately following the weather forecasts.

Weather Information

Weather forecasts are broadcast regularly, particularly at news times on Manx Radio courtesy of the Isle of Man Meteorological Office.
The frequencies used for Manx Radio are: 1368 KHz AM . 89-97.2-103.7 MHz Stereo FM Shipping Forecasts are broadcast daily by BBC Radio 4 (long wave 198 KHz 1515 M) at 05.55, 13.55, 17.50 and 00.33. Weather Forecasts are broadcast by BBC Radio 4 at 06.03, 06.55, 07.55, 08.58, 12.55, 17.55, 21.59 and 00.20. For further information on weather and tides in the Isle of Man, please contact the local Harbour Master in your area or Douglas Harbour Control on (01624) 686628.

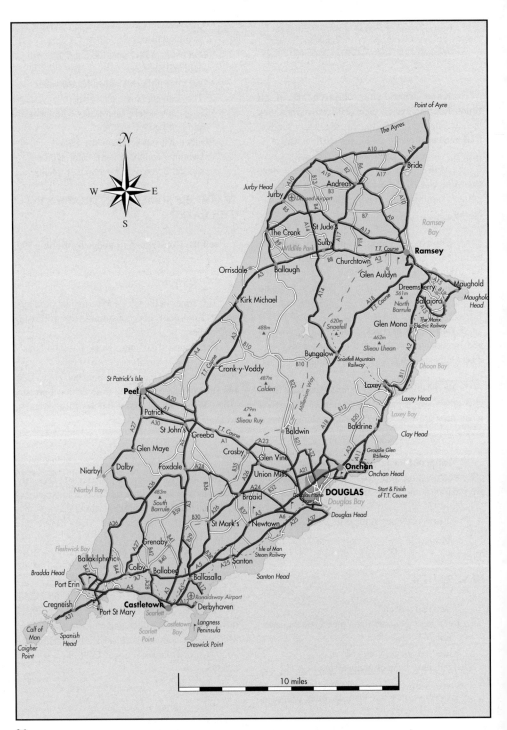

N
W E
S

Point of Ayre

The Ayres

A10   A16

Bride

B3   A17

Andreas   A10

Jurby Head
Jurby   A10
B13   B3
Disused Airport   A5
B5   B7   A9

St Jude's   Ramsey
The Cronk   A17   Bay
Sulby   A13
B8   T.T. Course
Churchtown   Ramsey
A3

Orrisdale   A3   Ballaugh   Glen Auldyn
Dreemskerry   A15   Maughold
561m   A18   Ballajora   Maughold
North   A13   Head
Barrule   The Manx
620m   Electric Railway
Kirk Michael   Snaefell
488m   A14   Glen Mona   462m
B10   Slieau Lhean   A2
T.T. Course   Bungalow   Snaefell Mountain   Dhoon Bay
Cronk-y-Voddy   B10   Railway   B11
487m   B22   Millennium Way
Colden   Laxey
St Patrick's Isle   479m   A18   Laxey Head
Peel   Slieau Ruy   Baldwin   A2   Laxey Bay
A1   A20   T.T. Course   B12   Clay Head
Patrick   A1   Greeba   A23   B21   Baldrine   A2
A30   St John's   A1   B20   Groudle Glen
A27   Crosby   Glen Vine   Railway
Glen Maye   B35   A2   Onchan
Niarbyl   Dalby   Foxdale   A24   Union Mills   A11   Onchan Head
Niarbyl Bay   483m   A26   A21   DOUGLAS   Start & Finish
South   A24   B32   Douglas Horse   of T.T. Course
Barrule   B30   Braaid   B27   Trams   Douglas Bay
B59   A26   Newtown   A5   A6   Douglas Head
St Mark's   B27   A25
Grenaby   B41   Santon
Fleshwick Bay   A27   B39   Isle of Man
Ballakilpheric   B42   B40   A25   Santon   Steam Railway
Bradda Head   Colby   B28   Santon Head
Port Erin   Ballabeg   A3
A5   A28   Ballasalla
Cregneish   A5   A3   Derbyhaven
Castletown   Ronaldsway Airport
A31   Port St Mary   Scarlett
Calf   Castletown   Langness
of   Scarlett   Bay   Peninsula
Man   Spanish   Point
Caigher   Head   Dreswick Point
Point

10 miles

The Isle of Man is generally portrayed as one resort, when the reality is that it is a number of separate resorts each offering distinctly different holiday opportunities. First time visitors are captivated by the variety of scenery and absorbed by the heritage of the Island. Within what is a relatively small land mass lies a range of views that would under normal circumstances take a visitor to the four corners of the British Isles for a comparison.

Sleepily journeying its way into the twentieth century the Island has developed a unique character all of its own. It is a land where rows of Victorian guesthouses sit happily with modern hotels and whitewashed farmhouses. The Isle of Man is a nation where old traditions still exist side by side with modern forward-seeking legislation, and where the smile and the quiet word live together in peaceful harmony.

Douglas

Douglas

Distances Ballasalla 9m, Castletown 12m, Laxey 8m, Peel 11m, Port Erin 15, Port St Mary 16m, Ramsey 16m.

The Isle of Man's front door is Douglas, nestling in the gentle curve of Douglas Bay and the best place to observe the Island's capital is from the top of Douglas Head. The whole of Douglas Bay, as far as Onchan Head, is spread out before you with the promenades and a seemingly endless line of hotels and guesthouses stretching away in the distance. Fringed by gardens to the front and with a backdrop of Snaefell, it is one of the most striking bays in Europe. On a fine summer's eve, Douglas wears its illuminations like a necklace. Thousands of jewel-like lights spread out over nearly two miles between the Heads of the

Bay, one of the greatest free shows on earth.

On the twin piers, millions of holiday makers have arrived in the elegant vessels of the Isle of Man Steam Packet Company. From these same piers, thousands of Manx have sailed away to a new life, while others departed by steamer to fight for King and country, some never to see their fair Isle again. Throughout the reigns of seven monarchs, this fine company has given over one hundred and sixty years of unbroken service to the Island. The harbour has witnessed lots of changes in the last decade and a half, after many years of standing still. How many people know that the King Edward Pier is the only public work or building named after the uncrowned sovereign? On leaving the gates of the Victoria Pier, how many people notice the memorial to the only working man in the history of the Island to have a public monument erected to his bravery? The "Dawsey" memorial commemorates the brave acts of David

SEFTON HOTEL

HIGHLY COMMENDED

The Sefton Hotel is more than an attractive, friendly hotel, it is the complete all year round Island holiday; bringing you the best possible inclusive travel, hotel facilities, good food and drink with an exciting range of holiday experiences to choose from - all at very competitive prices.

Relish the superb cuisine, prepared from the highest quality produce and served with real draught ales and quality wines at sensible prices. Whether you are in the mood for the carvery, grill room menu or a light afternoon snack, you can enjoy a succulent roast with all the trimmings, a vegetarian delight, a round of freshly made sandwiches, or something a little different in the **Far Pavilions** or the **Harris Coffee and Cocktail Lounge** or the new **Trams Bistro.**

The luxury **Fountain Health Club** includes a swimming pool, jacuzzi, relaxing poolside bar, gymnasium, steam rooms, saunas, sunbed rooms and a beauty therapy room.

The Tramshunters is the hotel's own CAMRA highly recommended pub with the widest range of real ales on the Island and beyond.

The Sefton is the perfect place from which to enjoy the Island. All 80 attractive ensuite bedrooms have satellite TV, Teletext, direct dial phones, hairdryers and tea/coffee making facilities. Our Family Suites provide you the luxury of privacy with a separate children's bedroom. In addition the new executive rooms also each have a sofa, fax, trouser press and iron with ironing board.

The Discovery Guide Visitor Centre *provides a fascinating selection of daily holiday options for you to choose from:*

Visit the Calf of Man seals, puffins, Manx shearwaters and choughs by boat, make your stage entrance through the hotel's secret door into the Victorian Gaiety Theatre, visit the world's oldest parliament, see the "Story of Mann" - all provide an insight into the history, culture, charm and beauty of this magic Isle.

INSTANT FULLY INCLUSIVE QUOTES AVAILABLE BY CALLING THE INFORMATION HOTLINE 663320

HARRIS PROMENADE . DOUGLAS . ISLE OF MAN . IM1 2RW . TEL 01624 626011 . FAX: 01624 676004
Internet address http://www.advsys.co.uk/sefton

"Dawsey" Kewley, a ropeman with the Isle of Man Steam Packet Company, who was reputed to have saved no less than twenty four men from drowning.

Emptying fresh water into the inner harbour is the Douglas River, which gives the town its name, but only flows from the eastern end of the National Sports Centre in the King George V Park. Two rivers, the Dhoo and the Glass join as one at this spot and the rest, as they say, is history! To learn more about the town a visit to the Museum is a must; any attempt to précis the story of Douglas would be derisory on the part of the author. It is far better for those who seek in-depth knowledge of the town to enjoy the process of information seeking at the Museum.

Postcards are an integral part of any holiday and the Island is lucky that it has a wide choice. Please remember though that besides our own currency, we have our own postage stamps. Several times each year the Isle of Man Post Office issues sets of new Definitive Stamps. These much sought after sets usually depict Island scenes or Manx connections. In 1995 for instance we had Thomas the Tank sets – take a close look at our real trains, there might be something familiar – other series included Fungi and the usual wonderful Christmas stamps. Planned for 1996 are sets depicting Island lighthouses, Manx Cats, a Europa set honouring famous women and a very special joint issue with the Irish Post Office representing the TT and some of the famous riders from across the Irish Sea. Stamp collecting has always been a popular hobby with young and old and the Island's stamps offer not only the opportunity to extend a collection but, in addition, they can be valuable souvenirs or presents from your holiday.

In case you need to phone home, Manx Telecom operate the same system of phones that

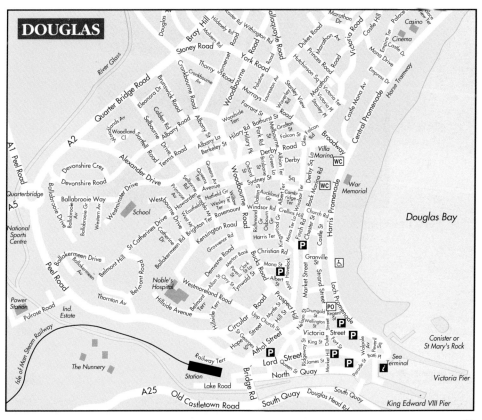

Don't Take A Chance With Your Holiday, Stay At The Island's Premier Hotel.

For a free Empress Hotel brochure and details of our All Inclusive Packages by air and sea, call now. Please quote Ref 10G2.

FREEFONE 0800 585060

THE
EMPRESS
HOTEL

A Better Understanding

HIGHLY COMMENDED

The Empress Hotel, Central Promenade, Douglas, Isle of Man. IM2 4RA. Telephone (0624) 661155 Fax (0624) 673554

you are used to back in the UK, however you will need to purchase one of their colourful phone cards for on Island use when using a Cardphone ... and they are nice to keep as souvenirs.

The world famous TT races in May/June each year, supported by the Manx Grand Prix in August/September, flood the Island with thousands of bikers and race enthusiasts. One of the best things about the races is the friendly club atmosphere that it generates.

For those who are unaware of the races and their historical connections with the Isle of Man, they have been running since 1907, and car races were even earlier than that! Steve Hislop's book "You Couldn't Do It Now!" is an excellent publication to help set out the background to the TT. Douglas has always played the leading role in the races and a visit to the TT Grandstand is a must, particularly at race times. Fans have their own particular favourite places to stay and return year after year, often becoming family friends with the hoteliers.

On Loch Promenade there are a number of well known family run hotels, all offering friendly personal service to their guests. Standing proudly in this beautiful terraced promenade and demonstrating the very best of Victorian Architecture, is the Stoneleigh Hotel. The skills used in getting the very best out of these graceful buildings is represented by the owners, Amanda and Ron. A value for money hotel with excellent facilities and special rates for parties. It is within easy walking distance of shops and many of the towns facilities and the whole bay can be seen from the Stoneleigh.

Almost next door, is the Cunard Hotel, which has all the facilities you would associate with a hotel of this size and there is no need to go out for an evening meal; they provide delicious dinners. The Quirk family offer reduced rates for children, groups and senior citizens, and if you are a golfer, you have chosen the right place to stay. A warm, friendly and welcoming hotel.

The Harris Promenade is home not only to the Gaiety Theatre but to the Sefton Hotel. This hotel is a firm favourite of the locals, a stamp of approval richly deserved and a sure indication of quality for the visitor. Naturally all the facilities normally associated with a hotel of this standing are there, such as a health club, coffee bar, restaurant with a magnificent choice of food, meeting rooms and a new conference centre with the most sophisticated and up to date support equipment. What singles out the Sefton from the crowd is their dedication to improve on their already significant facilities. In late summer 1995 they opened the instantly popular Trams Bistro and even more excellent developments can be expected. Immediately next to the front door of the theatre is the Discovery Guide Visitor Centre. The

centre provides all sorts of valuable information to the tourist including on Island specialist tours.

If self-catering is your taste in holiday accommodation then the conveniently situated Northwich Holiday Apartments should definitely be considered. These modern self-contained units have magnificent views of the sweep of Douglas Bay from headland to headland and you are assured of a warm welcome from the owners – the Gash family.

Moving further along we come to Central Promenade. Its most distinctive feature is the strikingly attractive Empress Hotel. The Empress has always been an industry leader and under new ownership it has been completely re-built. It had the distinction in 1992 of being the first hotel on the Isle of Man to be awarded the Five Crowns, Highly Commended rating; an award of which the management and staff are extremely proud. Justifying this high grading is easy, the hotel has every conceivable form of comfort and facility for their guests. Ranging from every one of the luxurious bedrooms with its own marble bathroom, to the health club with its indoor swimming pool

and on to the international cuisine of La Brasserie, the Empress gives full value for money and if you are not satisfied, they offer a money back guarantee of satisfaction. Now that is confidence for you!

In a different category to the Empress but matching it for the warmth of service is the family run Imperial Hotel. Shirley, Derek, Jeanne and David, with years of experience between them, manage this popular hotel. Home cooked meals, the bars, reception, bedrooms etc. all benefit from the hands on management of the family. Golfers find kindred spirits at the Imperial and if you want a group holiday, give them a ring, they can arrange all sorts of packages and deals. The sole aim of the Imperial team is to make your holiday a memorable one.

Just up the road stands the imposing Welbeck Hotel run by Peter, Hilda and Michael George. This is a hotel that always has its eye to the future and continually adds to its already impressive range of facilities. The Welbeck has an unrivalled reputation for friendliness and personal service and it just doesn't stop there; for example the beautiful

Conservatory Restaurant and bar ideally complement the hotel's conference suite. Reputed also for its excellent cuisine and the varied menu, the needs of the inner person are more than well catered for... in fact this hotel is just the place to relax in after a day of enjoying the Island's delights. The convenience of its location means the horse trams and other forms of public transport are close by. There is ease of parking and if you have any energy left, many of the town's amenities are just a short relaxing walk away.

One of the most high profile buildings on Douglas seafront is the Stakis Hotel & Casino, formerly known as the Palace, this popular hotel is enjoying a new lease of life as part of the world famous Stakis Group. The enthusiasm of the management and staff is second to none and if the visitor to our shores desires sophistication, quality cuisine and congeniality, then they need look no further. The range of entertainment facilities spread throughout the complex ensures that there is always something to suit everyone's taste. In late 1995 the hotel embarked on a massive multi-million pound refurbishment programme designed

Isle of Man Government Offices

to keep this hotel, casino, conference and leisure complex to the forefront of the tourist industry. The independent traveller, group or conference visitor are all important to the Stakis people, who will be only too happy to make all your arrangements for you.

Leaving Central Promenade behind, you come to the Queens Promenade. Total commitment to tourism is no stranger in the Isle of Man, particularly with many of the Douglas hotels. This dedication manifests itself in no better a place than the Regal Hotel on Queens Promenade. Run for many years by Colin and Carol Turner it guarantees choice menus using the best of local foods, extra amenities and many special offers. Send for their brochure, you will not be disappointed.

A hotel with a distinctive name in a very special spot is the Edelweiss. Set slightly back from the adjoining establishments, giving it the air of a haven from the bustle of everyday tourism, this hotel attracts you right from the moment that you first set eyes on it. Venture inside and ... yes that special feeling is still there. Owned and run by

The Welbeck Hotel
Comfort, Excellence & Friendliness

- All rooms en suite with bathroom, telephones, colour T.V. & tea & coffee making facilities.

- Seaview rooms available.

- Licensed bar & restaurant.

- Non-smoking area.

Treat yourself to
Luxury
Ask for one of our Executive Rooms for that extra . . .
Touch of Class

For brochure & package information ring:

FREEPHONE
0500 657808

- Conference & function suite.

- 100 yards from promenade.

- Minutes from town & financial centre.

- Lift to all floors.

- Personal fax machines available

Mona Drive (off Central Promenade), Douglas, Isle of Man
Tel: 01624 675663   Fax: 01624 661545

the Fleming family this is a uniquely different hotel.

Quite a number of public bars are along this end of town, the newly refurbished Queens Hotel being a good example. Selling Okell's bitter, they can't serve it fast enough in busy periods such as the TT, and if you like railway nostalgia, the Terminus Tavern is the place for you. The early morning sunshine brings out the early risers and many visitors sit outside their hotels enjoying the sun and reading their newspapers before eating a hearty Manx breakfast. Ideally situated for the Manx Electric Railway, just a few minutes' walk, there are equally no car parking problems at this end of the Promenade.

There are various methods of booking holidays to the Isle of Man, some of which have been mentioned elsewhere. Everymann Holidays is probably the largest Manx based company offering package holidays to the Island. Everymann is the Department of Tourism's very own tour operator and it combines the best of quality, value and choice to suit most budgets. The skilled staff working in Centaurmann House, Duke Street, have a comprehensive knowledge of the industry and are quickly able to match up your requirements to availability. Booking your holiday with Everymann benefits you in all sorts of ways. The size of the operation means that it can negotiate the best deals on your behalf with the carriers, you may also benefit from special discounts, reduced admissions and other concessions. Continual vetting of the product means that it maintains its high standards.

Douglas has many sides to it, far too many to describe in a publication of this nature. Informal entertainment there is in plenty with many of the pubs putting on musical entertainment, such as Casey's Cafe Bar. Formal entertainment in Douglas centres on the beautifully restored Gaiety Theatre. Throughout the year plays, pantomimes, concerts, last night of the proms and a veritable myriad of shows, delight audiences. Opened for its first performance in July 1900, the Gaiety soon won a place in the hearts of the locals and tourists, to the degree that it is now considered to be a national treasure. Frank Matcham, the famous Victorian

36

Victorian Horse trams serve on Douglas Promenade

theatre architect would be pleased that over ninety five years later his work still stands, largely unaltered, as a monument to his skills. In Government ownership, the management and staff are assisted by an enthusiastic band of helpers known as "The Friends of the Gaiety". Restoration work continues under the auspices of the Department of Tourism and Leisure and the "Friends", with the aim of returning the Gaiety to its original specifications in time to celebrate the theatre's centenary in the year 2000. This will make the Gaiety the only theatre in the British Isles to be restored in this manner and still working.

Enjoyment of your holiday is important and whatever the weather you can be assured that Summerland, the entertainment centre of Douglas will have something to suit everyone. New for 1996 is a supervised children's play area, known as "Manxland" which has to be seen to be believed. Mum and Dad can relax here whilst the children have fun and burn off their surplus energy, and you

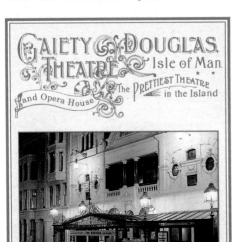
don't have to leave to find a snack or a drink, all can be found in the complex. Up to date films can be seen at Summerland's Piazza Cinema and each summer during the peak of the season, for six days a week, live family shows are performed.The sports facilities at Summerland are superb with roller skating, squash, badminton and table tennis being just a few of the participant sports that are available. All the sporting activities are supported with showers, saunas etc., but if you really want to cool off then a quick dash next door to the Aquadrome will do the trick. Open seven days a week, the thirty three metre main pool and trainer pool give hours of fun and are well supervised. In the summer fun sessions for the children are run in the afternoon – watch out for the octopus. For a real holiday treat, there are Turkish baths, saunas, sunbeds and an Aerotone Spa. Easy parking directly alongside the building.

One of the oldest companies in the Isle of Man and one which is very much involved in tourism is Okell's Limited, brewers of traditional bitter and mild beers. This fine old company has not let time stand still for them since they brewed their first beer in 1850 and they are now the proud owners of a new complex at Kewaigue on the outskirts of Douglas. The old Brewery in Falcon Street has not been abandoned however, conversion work at the end of 1995 turned it into a blue-ribbon off licence serving a whole range of beverages. One of the prime aims of the company is to ensure customer comfort and their refurbishment programme is continuous and on going. The Cat With No Tail is a brand new pub on the outskirts of Douglas, not too far from the Archibald Knox, the Manor and Onchan's Manx Arms, but don't worry where the pubs are as long as they are Okell's, they are all great, and easily accessible.

The famous Quarterbridge Hotel, the Bowling Green, and Molly's Kitchen and Tavern in Onchan, are but three of many hotels throughout the Island that have benefited from this visionary planning. Catering for generations of visitors, the brewery's name is synonymous with real ales which have largely disappeared from elsewhere in the British Isles. Their distinctive symbol is known by Islanders as the "Okell's Falcon". They have

Shopping in Douglas

numerous pubs, inns, and hotels spread all over the Island so, if you fancy a pint or two, look for the falcon and be assured of quality. A suggestion that might start you on the Real Ale Trail is to visit the "Barbary Coast". No, you have not left the Isle of Man, it is the local nickname for the pubs along the North Quay. Look out particularly for the British, Bridge, Claredon, Douglas and the Railway. The best pubs are not all confined to the touristy parts, try some of the older parts of town as well.

Not content with providing good hostelries the special brews that come out of Okell's can often become collectors items ... that is, as long as you can resist the temptation not to drink the whole batch. New for May 1996 will be Old Skipper Ale, brewed especially for the Traditional Boat weekend held over in Peel. A new stout also came on the market in October 1995; called Doolish Ale (after the town), it has quickly proved very popular. Honouring the fiftieth anniversary of the ending of W.W.II was Victory Ale and that old landmark Laxey Wheel did not miss out, with its very own production of Wheel Ale. Christmas is not forgotten so if you are over here for the festive season ask for a glass of St. Nick, it's bound to be full of good cheer. Good luck in your quest and remember, "Okell's, the taste that's stood the test of time".

The Island is proud of its food and playing a leading role in the food chain is the Isle of Man Fat Stock Marketing Association. Originally formed by local farmers this company has moved on to bigger things and besides its local customers now exports to the adjacent islands of England, Scotland, Wales and on occasions, further afield. Quality in all they produce are the bye words for the IOMFMA and with farm assured products they are able to meet the highest of EU standards, which is very much what the UK multiples require. Recent investments, totalling several million pounds in plant and machinery ensure that this go ahead company is well prepared to cope with the complexities of food production on a large scale. However the size of the operation has not sacrificed that special taste which is recognised as Manx grown and produced. Many restaurants feature dishes made from our delicious Manx meat, try it out for yourself ... you will not be disappointed.

No vacation is complete without taking photographs and visitors are always impatient to see the results. Ian and Monica Clark run Island Photographics, where those vivid reminders of the holiday can be processed. Their shop and laboratory are conveniently situated in Castle Street, not too far from the Gaiety Theatre. If you need any suggestions or assistance with your photographic requirements, ask at the shop – they will be only too pleased to help.

A close neighbour of Island Photographics is Brendan O'Donnell's Irish themed pub, brand new

and raring to welcome all. Shopping in Douglas is easy with the majority of shops situated behind Loch Promenade and running into Duke Street at the harbour end of town. Great plans are afoot for developing Douglas but the Strand Shopping Centre showing faith in the Island is already in full swing, and with several million shoppers visiting the "Strand", their confidence has been repaid. You can buy a full variety of goods here ranging from leading fashions, shoes, toiletries, babyware, books, electrical and household equipment, music and video tapes, greetings cards, fancy goods, toys, and even a new "hairdo".

By now you may have guessed that there is more to the Island than meets the eye. If it is your preference to learn in detail additional facts about the Isle of Man, then why not seek out the services of our renowned Blue Badge Guides. To gain their coveted Blue Badges is no easy task as each candidate must undergo thorough training and a stiff exam before qualifying. They operate on a freelance basis and although often committed to tour operators they are available for individuals and small groups. A trip with one of these experienced and knowledgeable folk is well worthwhile.

What does the future hold for Douglas in this ever-changing world of ours? This was a question posed a number of years ago in an attempt to plan the town's progress into the twenty first century. As a result, Douglas 2000 was born. Douglas 2000 is a Partnership of the Isle of Man Government, Douglas Corporation, the Chamber of Commerce and local companies working together to improve the environment and economy of the Island capital.

The Partnership has embarked upon a programme of more than one hundred tasks to make Douglas a successful town, well equipped for the twenty first century. Plans include a number of "Flagship" projects to bring about improvements to the shopping streetscape, promenade, Villa Marina, Villier's site, off street parking, a development zone and hopefully a town square, yacht harbour, and other exciting schemes some of which are already underway.

Only a short distance out of town on the road to Ballasalla lies one of the most exciting developments the Isle of Man has ever witnessed.

Douglas Seafront

The Mount Murray Hotel and Country Club at Santon could easily lay claim to an environmental prize for the way in which the whole complex sits in total sympathy with its surroundings. Prize-winning wouldn't stop there though, because this complex has brought a new dimension to holiday and business tourism that has probably never before been witnessed on the Island. The list of facilities within the hotel seems endless and if you add in such things as a conference centre,

championship golf course, driving range, tennis, squash and badminton courts then you can begin to realise why the Islanders themselves want to let the world know of this treasure in the Manx countryside. In fact seeing is believing ... don't miss the Mount Murray.

Public Amenities

Coastguard (Officer in Charge) (01624) 661664
General Post Office, Regent Street (01624) 686141
Douglas Corporation (Town Hall) (01624) 623021
Nobles (IOM) Hospital (01624) 663322
Police Station (01624) 631212

Emergency Only –
Fire, Police, Ambulance, Coastguard 999

43

Banks
Bank of Ireland (IOM), Christian Road (01624) 661102
Bank of Scotland (IOM), Prospect Hill (01624) 623074
Barclays, Victoria Street (01624) 682000
Isle of Man Bank, Athol Street (01624) 626232
Lloyds, Prospect Hill (01624) 638000
Midland, Victoria Street (01624) 684800
National Westminster, Prospect Hill (01624) 629292
Royal Bank of Scotland (IOM), Prospect Hill (01624) 629111
TSB Bank, Strand Street (01624) 673755

Building Societies
Alliance & Leicester (IOM), Prospect Hill (01624) 663566
Bradford & Bingley (IOM), Ridgeway Street (01624) 661868
Britannia (IOM), Victoria Street (01624) 628512
Leeds Permanent, Strand Street (01624) 626266
N & P Overseas, Strand Street (01624) 662244
Nationwide Overseas, Athol Street (01624) 663494

Victorian Gaiety Theatre, Douglas

Leisure Centres
Aquadrome (01624) 673411
Summerland (01624) 625511

Tourist Information
Current Flight Information (01624) 600600
Douglas Corporation Horsetrams (01624) 675222
Flight Information (01624) 824354
Harbour Control (01624) 686628
Isle of Man Railways (Steam & Electric) (01624) 663366
Isle of Man Steam Packet Company (01624) 661661
Isle of Man Transport (01624) 662525
Jersey European Airways (01624) 822162
Manx Airlines (01624) 824313
Museum, Manx National Heritage (01624) 675522
Ronaldsway Airport General Enquiries (01624) 821600
Tourist Information Centre, Sea Terminal (01624) 686766

Douglas

★Everymann HOLIDAYS

Start your Isle of Man Holiday

with Everymann 2 Nights from £69

The No1 for Sea/Air travel and accommodation

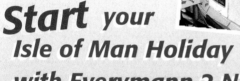

Everymann is the Isle of Man Department of Tourism's very own tour operator and offers the best combination of quality, value and choice to suit your pocket. We know the Island best and have welcomed over 170,000 visitors to our Island.

Everymann will make your Isle of Man holiday even more enjoyable. There's so much to choose from with Everymann and you'll also benefit from special discounts, reduced admissions and concessions on your travel in the Isle of Man.

Every hotel and guest house we offer has been vetted to ensure it represents a high standard in its category, with a large selection of accommodation from small friendly guest houses to high quality hotels.

We know you are looking forward to a trouble-free holiday or special weekend break. Going with Everymann Holidays gives you full security and the knowledge that you are booking with the Isle of Man holiday specialists. Why settle for less when you can go with Everymann and know you're getting value for money.

You will find all details including some very special offers in the Everymann Holiday Brochure. It's available from your local ABTA travel agent.

Booking with Everymann is simplicity itself. Sit back and enjoy a leisurely look through the Everymann Brochure. You'll find plenty to tempt you to visit the Isle of Man. Your local travel agent will be happy to make all the arrangements, check availability and help you to complete your booking form, or call the Everymann Central Reservations Office yourself on:

01624 629914

★Everymann HOLIDAYS

No1 for Travel and Accommodation

Send the coupon to: Everymann Holidays, Centaurman House, 20a Duke Street, Douglas, Isle of Man IM1 2RA **or telephone 01624 629914 or fax 01624 627514**

My special interest is:

- [ ] Family Holidays
- [ ] Heritage
- [ ] Tailor-made Holidays
- [ ] Over 55's Holidays
- [ ] Golf
- [ ] Romantic Weekend Breaks
- [ ] Walking
- [ ] Tours
- [ ] Fishing
- [ ] Special Activities
- [ ] Water sports

Name ....
Address ....
....
.... Postcode ....

★Everymann HOLIDAYS

Centaurman House, 20a Duke Street, Douglas, Isle of Man IM1 2RA
Reservations: 01624 629914 Fax: 01624 627514 Telex: 627793 MAN-INF-G

45

Ballasalla

Distances Castletown 3m, Douglas 9m, Laxey 17m, Peel 10m, Port Erin 6m, Port St Mary 7m, Ramsey 24m.

Ballasalla lies in the parish of Malew within the Sheading of Rushen. Flowing gently through the area is the Silverburn river and it is from this river that the village received its name. It is probable that *Salla* or *Sallach* was the ancient Gaelic name by which the early inhabitants knew the river; translated into English it means "the village of the sally or willow river". A more modern Gaelic translation of Silverburn is *Awin Argid* or Silver River.

The village is served by a regular bus service but during the summer months, nothing is better than to travel there by steam train. The line to Ballasalla is part of the 1873/4 built railway, connecting Douglas and Port Erin. However in 1986 a brand new station was built on the opposite side of the track to make way for an imposing set of offices which provide excellent employment opportunities for the people of the village. One of the beneficial aspects of business life in the Isle of Man is the efforts made by all sections of the economy to work together. At Ballasalla Station, you can witness this at first hand as you alight from the train onto the first new railway station to be built in the best part of a century. Crossleys the Accountants of Ballasalla are very proud to be the donors of this fine new addition to the railway. The office being situated alongside the track is of course a tremendous bonus for clients, who can pop out on the train to see their Accountants ... and the parking is pretty easy as well. If you need your finances taking care of, you might well find an exploratory meeting with these enthusiastic supporters of the Railway worthwhile.

Settled in early times Ballasalla has played its part in the making of Manx history. Within its boundaries lie the ruins of Rushen Abbey, said to have been founded in 1098 by Magnus, King of Norway. The building of the Abbey commenced in 1134 and although, as with many ancient sites, it was utilised over the centuries as a ready made source of building materials, much of the original buildings remain.

There have been many exciting discoveries made during excavations at the Abbey. Records show that a number of Kings and Abbots lie buried within its precincts and an excavation in the early part of this century discovered a skeleton of a man buried with a bronze figure representing Osiris an Egyptian God, which points to his having been a Crusader. The *Chronicon Manniae*, "Chronicles of Mann", a valuable reference work for the early history of the Island, were written at Rushen Abbey. Contained within the "Chronicles" is an account of the murder by a Knight called Ivar, of Reginald II, King of Mann. But the monks were busy in other areas as well, draining the land, straightening the course of the local rivers and streams, and generally influencing the way of life in those far off times. One valuable example of their handiwork still remains in every day use a few yards upstream from the Abbey Gardens. Known as the Monk's Bridge, its Gaelic name was *Crossag*, the little cross or crossing, it still carries people over the Silverburn river. Dating from the twelfth century and only 3 ½ feet wide, it is one of the finest examples of a packhorse bridge to be found anywhere in the British Isles.

Just a little further upstream from the bridge, the Silverburn is joined by the *Awin Ruy*, or Red River, whose bed is strewn with boulders as it flows down from *Rozefel*, Granite Mountain. Nowadays this mountain is called Stoney Mountain and it was from this source that much of the building materials came for the building of the new Douglas Breakwater in 1979. The Norsemen also recognised the colouring of the granite as it was exposed to the elements and knew it as *Rjoofjall*, Ruddy Mountain. Completing the short walk up from the Abbey to Silverdale Glen is a very pleasant experience, much loved by all ages and on the way ... look out for the Wishing Well.

There is much to recommend the visitor to Silverdale. Originally the site of the Creg Mill, its dam is now used as a boating lake. Utilising spare parts has always been a profitable pastime for the

Bluebells in the Spring

Manx and the water-powered roundabout is no exception. By using one of the old Foxdale mines water wheels and an ingenious method of gearing, generations of children "of all ages" have enjoyed themselves on this unique system. The beautifully kept cafe serves snacks and meals all day throughout a long season and there is often a special event to amuse everyone, no matter how old or young.

Ballasalla in the days of the Cistercians was very much a commercial centre for the Island and so it is today with Ronaldsway Airport falling within its boundaries. What the ancestors of today's villagers would think of the aeroplane is best left to the imagination! Ronaldsway lies a little to the South of the village and can be reached by bus or taxi. Although there is a railway halt nearby, this is now rarely if ever used. Given its name by the early Scandinavian visitors and meaning "Reginald's Ford", there were several Manx kings of this name too! Within the original Norse spelling of the name, *Rognvaldsvao*, the *vao* would have referred to the tarbet across the neck of Langness which was used as the pathway when the Viking longboats were dragged over to the other side of the peninsula and the quieter waters of Castletown Bay. Ronaldsway is also reputed to be the site of King Orry's castle and it has been the scene of many a battle. After the execution of *Illiam Dhone*, his estate of Ronaldsway was sequestrated but later returned to his family, and the last man to include Ronaldsway in his title was

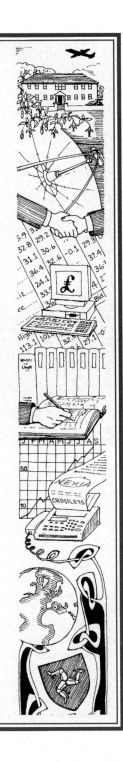

a direct descendant of William Christian, Rear-Admiral Sir Hugh Christian who was elevated to the peerage but who died just before the patent reached him.

Public Amenities
Ballasalla Post Office (01624) 822531
Police Station (not continuously manned) (01624) 822543, (01624) 631212

Banks
Isle of Man Bank, Station Road (01624) 822503

Leisure Centre
Silverdale Glen Cafe (01624) 823474

Derbyhaven

Heading out beyond the airport perimeter the car driver can easily find the way to the picturesque hamlet of Derbyhaven. There is an occasional bus service to this part of the Island but the casual traveller is advised to check with the bus company (Manx National Transport). Well utilised by small boats, it no longer has any commercial shipping activities, but at the time of the Vikings and their medieval successors, it was a thriving port.

The old smelthouse at Derbyhaven, whose remains are still visible, probably dates from around 1711. It was here that Blacksmith John Wilks – two former Governors of the Bank of England are directly descended from him – made the Island's first penny coins, an action which Tynwald authenticated by making them legal tender. There is solid evidence to prove that exclusively Manx coinage was minted by one John Murrey a merchant of Douglas in 1668 and he appears to have been the owner of the Derbyhaven Mint. Incidentally, it seems that the rate of exchange decided upon in 1709 by James II, tenth Earl of Derby, when he authorised a new issue was fourteen Manx pennies to twelve British, but by the time that the only Manx money issued under Atholl rule came on the market, the rate of exchange was only half, and that was in favour of the British coinage.

The sandy turf of the Langness Peninsula is home to the famous Castletown Golf Links. There cannot be many hotels where you can step out of the front door onto the first tee and play on a world class golf course.

Close by the ruins of the smelthouse is the 10th hole and it was here, 153 years before it was transferred to Epsom Downs in 1780, that the famous Derby horse race originated. It seems that the seventh Earl of Derby wished to encourage the breeding of Manx horses and as an incentive presented a cup to be won in open competition. One stipulation he did put on the race was that only those horses that had been foaled within the Island or on the Calf of Man were allowed to be entered. The Manx horses of that period were small and very hardy, renowned for their speed, surefootedness and stamina. It may well be that prior to the Derby the only time horses were in competition was after a wedding when the guests raced back to the bridegroom's home to claim the honour of breaking the bride-cake over the bride's head, as she entered her new home!

Langness is very well known for its wildlife and by far the best way to view it is to walk. There is a variety of bird life, watch out for the skylarks especially, and on a pleasant summer's evening nothing can be better than to watch the seals swimming about or just taking life easy at Dreswick Point, the southern-most tip of the Isle of Man. Please do not be misled by the sometimes peaceful waters, they conceal jagged rocks which have claimed many lives. A short distance from the lighthouse and in line with the Herring Tower is Tharastack Gulley, where in 1853 the crew of the Plymouth schooner "Provider" perished. These poor souls were buried in sight of the wreck and their burial-place site is marked by a nearby natural tombstone of rock carved with the vessel's name and the date of her loss.

Castletown

Distances Ballasalla 3m, Douglas 9m, Laxey 20m, Peel 13m, Ramsey 26m, Port Erin 5m, Port St Mary 7m.

The ancient Capital of Mann for several centuries, Castletown has a charm all of its own. Sited at the edge of a long extinct and almost untraceable volcano, the town was guardian for the Manx in times of war and peace. The virtual end to commercial seaborne traffic came in the 1970's but in more recent times there has been a revival in business, with a number of commercial activities based on the finance sector being located there. It is the only town in the parish of Malew and as a result of long association with the seat of government, visitors to the area will soon pick out many anglicised names around the town and its vicinity. Names to look out for are Bowling Green, Great Meadow, Paradise (now Ellerslie and the former home of General Cuming who was with

Castletown Harbour

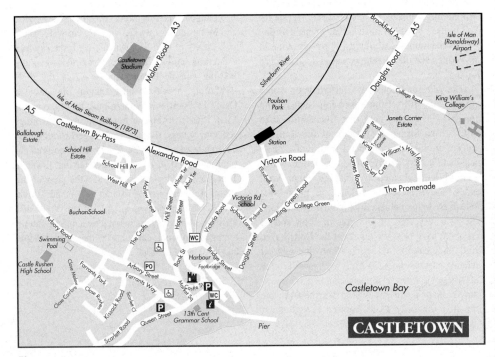

Wolfe at Quebec), Red Gap, Witches Mill and the Rope Walk. Many of the homestead names in the proximity such as *Grenaby*, *Tosaby* and *Orrisdale* testify to the fact that Castletown and its surrounding area were well colonised by the Norsemen.

Journeying to Castletown is made easy by the regularity of the year round bus service and the steam railway which operates in both directions several times a day during the summer. Well signposted roads offer alternative approaches to the town. The narrow streets of Castletown evoke memories of yesteryear and a pleasant time can be had by merely strolling around the town, but with so much else to see it deserves a long visit.

Finishing its journey from the highlands of the parish the Silverburn gently empties into the picturesque harbour, pausing, almost as if for a last look around, as it flows under the Apostles Bridge. It's easy to work out where the bridge gets the name from! There is one other river in the area, which makes its entry into the sea just on the western edge of the town at Red Gap. It rejoices in the unusual name of the "Dumb River", so called because it is literally dumb and makes no sound, flowing across flat country throughout its entire course.

The harbour without doubt can give much pleasure to any sailor, prospective or otherwise, and it is highly recommended that a visit be made to the Nautical Museum. Containing much nautical memorabilia of bygone eras, the star of the display is the eighteenth century armed yacht "The Peggy", still in her original boathouse and only rediscovered by accident in 1935, a hundred years after her owner Captain George Quayle's death. Castletown harbour is built on a shelf of lava, clearly seen at low water. Millions of years ago during the formation of the Isle of Man a volcanic eruption laid the foundations for the landscape much as we now see it. For those interested, a stroll along the shoreline towards Scarlett Point will be rewarded with a view of past volcanic activity. Wind, tide and rain over the aeons have exposed the volcano's surviving plug. Close by there is a Nature Trail and Visitors Centre (Open Wednesdays to Sundays 2 – 5pm., mid May until

mid September).

With practically all the ancient buildings in the town grouped around the harbour and to the seaward side of the Castle, there is a virtual treasure trove for the serious historian and casual visitor alike. There is for instance the old Castletown Grammar School, built originally as the ancient capital's first church in approximately 1200; it played an important part in later centuries in the education of the young people of the Island. Nearby is the old garrison church of St. Mary's built in 1826 to replace Bishop Wilson's church of 1698, saved in recent times from dereliction and now a thriving business house. In 1777 John Wesley, the founder of Methodism on paying his first visit to the Island, preached in front of the Castle and noted in his journal of the 30th June, that "A more loving, simple-hearted people than this I never saw".

A walk up from the outer harbour through the narrow streets will bring you to the old House of Keys building, which for a long time, from 1709, was the seat of government until population and commercial pressures forced the Keys to decamp

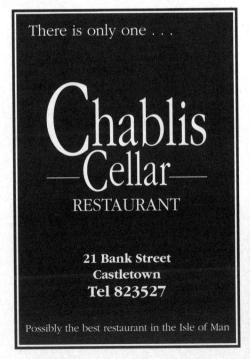

Castletown Harbour

to Douglas in 1869. The builder's receipt shows that the building was constructed for the princely sum of £83-5s-6½d.

Standing sentinel over Castletown and the southern lowlands is Castle Rushen. Dating from Norse times, its huge limestone structure is visible for miles around. This imposing fortress is one of the most complete of its type in the whole of the British Isles, and if its walls could speak, they would tell of mystery and intrigue, murder and mayhem, kings and consorts, and the many important events that have changed and moulded the life of this Island. A close inspection of the staircases at Castle Rushen shows that they spiral to the right, thus forcing any attackers to use their left hand to grip their swords whilst the defenders were free to use their right hand. The Castle is a living building, decorated in authentic style and giving the visitor an instant impression of life in medieval/ seventeenth century Manxland. It is still a working castle hosting High and Low courts and at regular intervals witnessing weddings within the precincts of its courthouse.

A visit to the market square produces a scene

hardly changed from the 1800's. In the centre of the square stands Smelt's Memorial, erected in 1838 to honour a Governor – Cornelius Smelt 1805 to 1832 – and to this day still incomplete. The good folk of Castletown refused to contribute for a statue to grace the column and for the first few years after it was erected it became known as the "Castletown Candlestick". Today it gives sterling service as a traffic roundabout ... have a look at the plaque on the side, you will find it interesting. Across the way from the Smelt Memorial and close to the George Hotel, is the former home of Captain John Quilliam RN who fought at the Battle of Trafalgar and saved HMS "Victory" from destruction by rigging a jury (temporary) rudder at the height of the fighting. Looking down on the square is a clock presented to the Island by Queen Elizabeth I. It has only ever had one finger and is still going strong after almost four hundred years.

You may feel a need for sustenance after walking around the town for an hour or so, and there is no better place for refreshments than the Chablis Cellar. Offering cuisine par excellence this delightful restaurant is one of the Island's finest and if you miss having lunch there, come back later for dinner you will not be disappointed.

The outskirts of Castletown have almost as much history as the town itself. Lying to the East of the old metropolis is King William's College, a long time site of public school education, its great central tower dominating the landscape. The idea of the College probably first surfaced in a letter from the seventh Earl of Derby, *Yn Stanlagh Mooar*, to his son Charles but due to the subsequent outbreak of the English Civil War, his idea did not come to fruition until 1833. Facing the school is Hango Hill, where *Illiam Dhone* met his end. The Norse name for the hill was *Hangaholl*, or Hill of Hanging, and William Christian was the last person to be executed there. It is also a very important archaeological site. The ruins are in fact of a blockhouse built by the seventh Earl at the time of the unrest in England.

To the West of the town is the Balladoole estate centred on the fine Balladoole House, the home of the Stevensons for many hundreds of years. There is evidence in the Manx Museum that at least six generations of the family lived on the estate prior to a mention in the manorial records of 1511. John Stevenson was the Speaker of the House of Keys, 1704 to 1738 and his name should forever be remembered by the Manx Nation for the manner in which he led the Keys in their patriotic struggle against the tenth Earl of Derby. Bishop Wilson called him "The Father of his Country" and at one time he was imprisoned in Castle Rushen for championing the rights of his fellow countrymen. The last bearer of the family name was Sir Ralph Stevenson, who retired as British Ambassador to Egypt in 1955 and who suffered great agonies as the British, French and Israelis stormed ashore at the time Nasser appropriated the Suez Canal just a year later.

To the West of Balladoole is *Poyll Vaaish*, which is easily reached by car or on foot from Castletown by following the coastal footpath *Raad ny Foillan*, The Road of the Gull. The walk from Castletown hosts marvellous views of the surrounding countryside. A particular favourite of the locals is the panoramic vista looking northwards as the low hills of the coastal areas roll ever

upwards to the central mountain range, with *Snaefell* visible in the far distance. Just after dropping down from the basaltic Stack of Scarlett the walker comes upon a small quarry which produces high quality black marble. It was from this source that Bishop Wilson gifted the stone from which the steps of St. Paul's Cathedral were made, and again in recent years replaced when worn out. Close by the Stevenson's ancestral home there is the site of a Viking Ship burial mound and this together with a number of important archaeological sites makes a visit to the area well worthwhile.

At the point where the coastal footpath joins the main road (A5) is the area known as *Poyll Vaaish* or translated into the English "Death Pool or Bay of Death". Probably the name is derived from the black marble which comprises the sea bed in the vicinity and the ripples of lava clearly seen above the low water mark. There are legends galore about this corner of the Island. Stories of shipwrecks, pirates, and looters abound, and on a wet and windy night it is not too difficult to imagine the calls of distressed sailors wafting shoreward on the breeze. Strandhall which lies to the right when heading on South has a spring flowing down onto the shore and legend tells that, although the source of the spring lies many feet above sea level, it is reputed to be a salt water spring with petrifying powers. Indeed at extremely low tides and particularly after a storm has moved the sands, the remains of a large petrified forest can sometimes be seen.

Rounding *Baie ny Carrickey*, The Bay of the Rocks, the road follows the water's edge passing as it does the Treen lands of *Kentraugh*, "Shore End", the home of the Gawne family for centuries. There are fine sands here with excellent boating waters but as ever please watch the weather and tides, the sea can play strange tricks on the unsuspecting. At the West end of the bay lies *Gansey*, this Scandinavian name means Magic Bay. Peaceful now but in the past, the scene of many a struggle between the forces of law and order and the farmers and fishermen of Mann. It is interesting to note that in the short distance between Castletown and *Kentraugh* the traveller has moved across three parishes, Malew, Arbory and into Rushen.

Public Amenities
Castletown Post Office (01624) 822516
Castletown Commissioners (Town Hall) (01624) 825005
Harbour Master+s Office (01624) 823549
Police Station (not continuously manned) (01624) 822222, (01624) 631212

Banks
Barclays, Market Square (Central Switchboard) (01624) 682000
Isle of Man Bank, Market Square (01624) 822503
TSB Bank, Market Square (01624) 822755

Leisure Centre
Southern Swimming Pool, Arbory Road (01624) 823930

Tourist Information
Castle Rushen (01624) 823326
Castletown Station (Seasonal) (01624) 822275

Port St Mary

Distances Ballasalla 7m, Castletown 4m, Douglas 16m, Laxey 24m, Peel 16m, Port Erin 2m, Ramsey 28m.

Ahead of you lies the pretty fishing village of Port St. Mary, which is the English form of the Gaelic *Keeill Moirrey*, more commonly referred to as *Purt-le-Moirrey*. The impressive backdrop to this village is the Mull Peninsula with its steep slopes and fields rolling right down into the village itself. Part of the land has been turned into a fine 9-hole golf course which is popular with locals and visitors alike.

At one time a thriving fishing port, home for both local and Scottish vessels, it now hosts a factory, processing the local shellfish delicacy known as Queenies. The harbour is now full of fine yachts and leisure vessels of all types. The breakwater gives good shelter and its deepwater berths prove popular with visiting sailors and the few remaining fishing vessels. The inner pier, the Alfred Pier, named after a previous Duke of Edinburgh who laid the foundation stone in 1882, shelters the smaller craft and is a very picturesque part of the Port. Clustered round the harbour are old Manx cottages – thatched roofs having long ago given way to Manx slate – transporting the visitor back in time to a more relaxed way of life. The newer part of Port St. Mary lies above the sandy beach of Chapel Bay where generations of children have learned to swim and to build their first sandcastles. Linking the harbour and the bay is a fine walkway winding its way close to the water's edge. The local pubs once frequented solely by the men of the fishing fleet, now garner their harvest from the yachting fraternity and the passing tourist trade.

Perwick, owes its name to the old Scandinavian word for Harbour Creek. In very recent times the hotel that once stood at the edge of the cliff has been developed for private housing but the beach is still worth a visit, particularly if you have more than a passing interest in geology. There

Port St Mary

is a very noticeable "fault" on the South East side of Perwick Bay which clearly shows where the carboniferous and slate rocks meet under an overlay of glacial clay. Until the beginning of this century there were the remains of a fort to be seen on the shore. Now the best play area for the young ones is the rocky pools and small caves at the foot of the cliffs.

Climbing out of the Port, the next village is *Fistard* which sits high on the hillside above Perwick Bay. *Fistard* gives its name to the Treen which includes Port St Mary and is the Scandinavian for Fish's Garth or Farm. Perhaps it is the fact that the village and its near neighbour the Howe are perched high above the world below that accounts for the timelessness of the area. Little seems to have changed as the years roll by and even though the villagers often earn their living elsewhere, the hustle and bustle of modern life is left behind at the foot of the hill. The student of history researching the OS maps of last century will see that the Howe has slightly changed

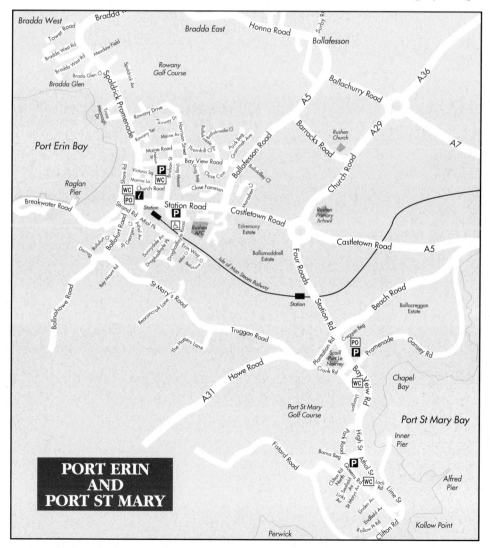

PORT ERIN
AND
PORT ST MARY

Port St Mary

position. The Howe is one of the few English place names on the Isle of Man and is probably from the meaning of hill. So as not to offend the good neighbours of the Howe, we had better leave the village where it is!

Public Amenities
Harbour Master's Office (01624) 833206
Police Station (not continuously manned) (01624) 833222, (01624) 631212
Port St Mary Commissioners (Town Hall) (01624) 832101
Port St Mary Post Office (01624) 833113

Cregneash

L eaving the narrow lanes of Fistard and the Howe behind, the A31 climbs still higher up Mull Hill to the village of *Cregneash*. Don't worry if your map refers to it as *Cregneash*, the first spelling is the Gaelic way. It means Rock of Ages. The village is the oldest in the Isle of Man and part of it forms the Folk Museum run by Manx National Heritage. The thatched cottages nestle in

and around a sleepy hollow and the views of the Calf of Man and the Sound are stunning. If you like agriculture, the Museum's working farm is a must and you may also be lucky and see the thatcher at work. As with the two lower villages, the people of the Mull Peninsula cling to old-time customs and have been little influenced by the march of progress.

Across the way from the "modern" village lies the remains of an older village. The Mull Circle, in Manx *Meayl*, meaning Bald or Bare Hill, dates back to the late Neolithic or early Bronze Age. Used primarily as a prehistoric burial place, it is unique in archaeology terms, combining the circle form with six pairs of cists, each pair having a passage between which radiates outwards. The prehistoric village was below the circle and hut foundations and other relics were discovered on the site. In case you think the Martians have landed nearby, they haven't! What you are actually seeing on the hilltop above the village is a Radiobeacon that just happens to look like a flying saucer ... from a distance! Trans Atlantic flights home in on this beacon when making their landfall from the new world. The huddle of buildings nearby house a similar system for Irish Sea shipping. A walk on

Cregneash

past the beacons brings you to the Spanish Head Manx National Trust area, home to the incredible Chasms – described more fully in the Cliffs section of the Guide.

If you missed a snack at Cregneash, don't worry, just carry on down the hill, and Terry Jackson and his team will ensure that you are well fed and watered at the Sound Cafe, where they generate their own wind powered electricity. The culinary delights of this cafe have a reputation second to none for home made meals and snacks ... try the local crab dishes! Give yourself plenty of time here as it is a number one beauty spot for the Island and is listed amongst the top 10 scenic spots of Great Britain. Come prepared with binoculars, on a calm day you might catch sight of the Basking Sharks as they cruise past or the Grey seals sunbathing on Kitterland. The cafe is well stocked with souvenirs and books by local authors.

The Sound – the Land's End of Mann – is a good place to stretch stiff limbs or as a starting off point for more energetic exercise. Try the walk back to Port St Mary or on to Port Erin, it is well worth it.

Calf of Man and the Sound

Port Erin

Port Erin

Distances Ballasalla 6m, Castletown 5m, Douglas 15m, Laxey 23m, Peel 16m, Port St Mary 2m, Ramsey 28m.

Whichever way you approach Port Erin, be it from the North, South, East or by sea from the West there is one common denominator, the views are impressive. Port Erin translated means either Lord's Port or Iron Port and in the Manx Gaelic it is written as *Purt Chiarn*. Latter day smugglers came to know Port Erin very well, using the solitude of the bay to mask their activities and kept safe from observation by the steep hills and perpendicular cliffs surrounding the village. In modern times the village became the playground of the Lancashire mill owners and their employees, and it is no wonder the peace and contentment that the visitors of the early part of the twentieth century experienced could well be described as "far from the madding crowd".

Crowning the swirl of the bay are four hotels owned by the Port Erin Hotels Group. The majestic stance of these 2, 3 and 4 crown hotels is reflected by the very able team led by Sue Gowing. For sheer hard work and dedication to their guests these hotels – the Countess, Princess, Imperial and Royal – have no equal and much of their business is derived from the year on year return of their happy visitors. Besides the standard facilities offered there are many extras such as golf and tennis nearby and what's important at no additional cost! The planning by the team that goes into ensuring your holiday goes well is legendary within the Island's tourist industry. Port Erin Hotels have a simple philosophy, which is devoted to ensuring that no matter if you stay with them as an individual, a family or a group, or for however long, all receive first class care and attention. No need to worry about complicated booking arrangements, one telephone call or fax to their in-house company Goldstar Travel Services does it all, and you can already begin to savour an enjoyable holiday.

Sharing the Promenade with the larger hotels is the very attractive Regent House Guest House. This elegant guesthouse is just the place to relax in and if you have special dietary needs, don't worry they can be catered for. This guest house is the epitome of all that's good about Manx accommodation.

In a prime position, the Falcon's Nest Hotel offers personal attention that is special to a family run establishment, and Mr and Mrs Potts and their team are no exception to the rule. Fine foods sourced on the Island, real ales and over 100 varieties of whisky to choose from produce a climate of good will ... and the views and sunsets are thrown in for free. If it's local atmosphere you seek then this is the place to stay or if you are visiting the village why not drop in for a drink, snack, meal or just a plain old piece of conversation with the locals, they will be delighted to meet you. It's a popular place and very handy to the bus and railway stations. Built by the philanthropist William Milner, it is the oldest hotel in the village and in earlier years the British Prime

PORT ERIN HOTELS

Minister William Gladstone stayed there. The Potts family commitment to value for money for their guests extends to free transfers from the airport or sea terminal and children under 16 can share their parent's room free of charge.

Situated at the head of an almost landlocked bay, guarded to the North by lofty Bradda Head and the Castle Rocks and Mull Peninsula to the South, Port Erin offers a sheltered play area in most weathers. Pretty white painted cottages trim the inner edge of the bay, bordered by grassy banks, rising up to a more formal promenade fronting a traditional line of seaside hotels. As with all seaside towns there are a variety of places to eat and drink. When you spot the Okell's sign you can usually sort out lunch or snack requirements; try the Station or the Haven. Port Erin is a very photogenic place by virtue of its symmetry with sea, sand, cliffs, hill and heather. Stir into that combination, shadows and brilliant sunsets often framed by the Mountains of Mourne, and you have a picture painted by God's own hand. If you have left your sketch book at home, don't worry! There is a nice little bookshop in the village which can

supply most forms of art equipment, just in case the mood to sketch or paint creeps up on you Holidays are usually the only time most busy people have to catch up on their reading and they also have a good selection of books to choose from. If you would like some culture whilst on holiday, check with the Erin Arts Centre, they frequently hold musical and artistic events.

Over one hundred years ago the excellence of the waters offshore from Port Erin was recognised and the Marine Biological Station was established at the seaward end of the bay. Still operating, now as an annex to Liverpool University, it is well known and respected throughout the marine world. Many famous experts consult the Station and no less a personage than the late Emperor of Japan, a renowned marine life specialist, frequently made contact – a tradition maintained by the present Emperor who has in fact visited in person. Directly opposite this seat of learning are the remains of a breakwater started in 1864 and meant to turn the bay into the national harbour of refuge. William Milner of Bradda Head fame was a staunch supporter of the breakwater and he along with everyone else on the Island would have felt a great sense of loss when in one single night in January 1884, it was destroyed in a storm.

One of the more famous residents of Port Erin in recent years has been World Champion Formula 1 and Indianapolis Champion, Nigel Mansell. Nigel loved the unhurried way of life on the Island and particularly in Port Erin. He always got great pleasure from the fine golf course. A son of Port Erin who made his way to the far side of the earth seeking fame and fortune was William Kermode, born in 1775. Taking up a grant of land in Van

Port Erin

Diemen's Land, now of course known as Tasmania, he amassed a fortune and contributed valuable service to the Tasmanian Legislative Council. A story from that far off land tells of how Kermode was once ambushed in his coach by two bush rangers who demanded his money or his life! Reacting faster than the robbers, he smacked their heads together, bound them up and drove to Hobart where the law recognised them as the most dangerous men of the day. Robert Quayle Kermode, the son, also did sterling work in Tasmania having a large say in the abolition of the Australian State's convict status.

Public Amenities
Harbour Master's Office (01624) 833205
Police Station (not continuously manned) (01624) 832222, (01624) 631212
Port Erin Commissioners Office (Town Hall) (01624) 832298
Port Erin Post Office (01624) 833119

Banks
Barclays, Station Road (Central Switchboard) (01624) 682000
Isle of Man Bank, Station Road (01624) 822503

Tourist Information
Port Erin Bus Depot (01624) 833125
Port Erin Railway Station (Seasonal) (01624) 833432

Colby & Ballabeg

To the East of Port Erin in the flat lands of Arbory are the villages of Colby and Ballabeg. *Colby*, Kolli's Farm, stands at the entrance to the delightful Colby Glen. A walk up the Glen takes the visitor alongside a babbling brook as it runs its lower course through wooded glades and higher still where the gorse is a riot of colour. Further up the Glen there are the remains of *Keeill Catreeney* and a burial ground. The ancient St Catherine's or Colby Fair used to be held here. Nearby there is *Chibbyrt Catreeney*, Catherine's

Port Erin

Beautiful country views

Well, and it was woe betide anyone who drank from here as they were afflicted with an unquenchable thirst for ever. Incidentally, if you are thirsty, the Colby Glen Hotel is nearby and will look after your needs more than adequately, and you can have a very nice meal there.

Another fair, which has survived to this very day is *Laa Columb Killey*, St Columba's Day Fair. Held in a special field in either Colby or Ballabeg at the end of June each year, it attracts people from all over the Island and gives a glimpse of country life as it used to be. *Ballabeg* is on the ancient quarterland and the village is named from the 1511 Manorial Roll as Begson's Farm. The area is very much rural and the quiet sheltered lanes are lined by foxgloves and wild fuschia. If you are in a vehicle, pull over and park, enjoy what the ramblers hear ... the occasional bleat of a sheep or the song of a bird, the rustle of the ferns and grasses as the breezes keep them moving in a fan like action. Weedkillers and pesticides are not used on the Manx hedgerows and it is still possible to see wild flowers which have disappeared from other parts of the British Isles due to irresponsible husbandry of the countryside. The lanes of Arbory and the neighbouring parishes of Malew and

Rushen play host to a multitude of plant and animal life.

Countryside holidays are becoming more and more popular and if your ideal is a get away from it all holiday, then Ronague Holiday Homes might offer the solution. This organisation has two delightful holiday houses in the South, both with magnificent views over miles of the surrounding countryside. One, a secluded farmhouse straddles a geological fault thus giving it an enviable elevation whilst the other a converted Methodist chapel lies further up the mountainside and offers unsurpassed panoramic views.

The church has always played an important part in the life of the South of the Island and none more so than Kirk Arbory. Built in 1757 the present church has an oak beam supporting the roof which belonged to two previous churches. There is an inscription on the beam mentioning Thomas Radcliffe, Abbot of Rushen and it seems to refer to the Stanley crest of an Eagle and Child. The grave of Captain Quilliam of H.M.S. *Victory* and Trafalgar fame is in the churchyard. Along the road from the church towards Castletown is Friary Farm. Clearly visible from the road are the remains of the Friary of Bemaken, founded by the Grey

ISLE OF MAN POST OFFICE

COLLECT MANX STAMPS!!

Niarbyl

Friars in 1373. The holy men were assisted in its completion by stone masons who were on the Island to do work on Castle Rushen. Employed by William de Montacute and later his son, the masons were on the move around Britain strengthening castles and fortifications between 1368 and 1374. Two Ogham stones were found on the site and are now in the safe keeping of the Manx Museum. The stones are inscribed in the ancient British and Irish alphabet Ogham which was used for writing Irish from the fourth or fifth century A.D. to the early seventh century.

Glen Maye, Dalby & Niarbyl

lion Muigh, Yellow Glen, is a village sitting on steep hillsides at the bottom end of the mining glens of Glen Mooar and Glen Rushen. On beyond the village the river plunges over a series of waterfalls, before finishing its dash to the sea between two hundred foot high, gorse and heather clad cliffs. It is easy to see that the village of Glen Maye owes its existence to the farming and mining industries and the good efforts

of the householders have ensured that it has retained its old character. A favourite watering hole for locals, and the tourists who discover it, is the Waterfall Hotel. On a fine summer's eve a pleasant hour or two can be whiled away in the Inn and the beautiful glen offers a delightful opportunity to walk your lunch or evening meal off.

Niarbyl, or to give it its Manx name *Yn Arbyl*, The Tail, on account of the long reef jutting out from the shoreline, is an ideal place for picnics; the superb views to the North and South still thrill, no matter how many times you see it. The isolation of this part of the Island can best be seen from here. The full grandeur of the south western coast can clearly be contemplated, with the massive cliffs stretching away southward in a series of giant headlands and bays before Bradda Head briefly interrupts the flow. The Mull Hills continue the vista and from this angle it almost seems as if the Calf of Man is joined to the main island. Wonderful walking country.

Foxdale

Foxdale means Waterfall Dale and with the area containing many streams, it is aptly named. Once upon a time it was a famous centre for lead mining and from the three hundred or so tons of ore that were mined each month, some fifteen to twenty ounces of silver per ton were extracted. Closed down for good in the early part of the century, many of the miners emigrated to the colonies, and it has taken years for the village to begin to recover some of its lost prosperity. Times are improving and the economic life of Foxdale is slowly returning the area to its former glory. By the way, if you are a keen fisherman, call in and see Bill Duquemin, in his shop, he is a "mine" of information on fishing. Bill's refreshing style of customer relations assures a welcome to all. Even if you are not a fishing type he is a helpful guide on all manner of subjects.

Many of the farms in the area are branching out into tourism by converting outbuildings and old cottages to self-catering use. On such farms, guests can live in close contact with the daily routine of a working farm and if the children like animals then their stay will be idyllic. The rural location belies the fact that the main towns and beauty spots are only a few minutes' drive away and in the evening if you feel like a good pint or glass of cheer, the Baltic is only a short walk away.

Peaceful country lanes

Peel

Distances Ballasalla 10m, Castletown 13m, Douglas 11m, Laxey 19m, Port Erin 16m, Port St Mary 16m, Ramsey 16m.

Peel has to be to the forefront in everyone's touring plans of the Island. Taking its name from the castle, the name appears in the 1231 Papal Bull of Gregory IX as *Pile*, which was an alternative name for *Inis Patrick*, St Patrick's Isle. Peel, in its abbreviated form, only came into everyday use in the nineteenth century, although it was being used at the beginning of the eighteenth century. The Gaelic for the city is *Purt ny Hinshey*, Island Town. Always a centre of civilisation, Peel is so steeped in history that to attempt to do more than give a flavour of the place would be to commit an injustice. Do give plenty of time in your programme to take in the sights and atmosphere of this ancient city, for that is what it is, being the proud possessor of a Cathedral down through the centuries. The present Pro-Cathedral in the centre of Peel is a fine building, see it for yourself.

Exciting developments are taking place in Peel as Manx National Heritage continue their programme of telling the "Story of Mann" through numerous sites around the Island. In the case of Peel, a multi-million pound commitment to the history of the Island is unfolding and soon the city will have a building displaying our treasures and heritage to a standard equalling Jorvick, the Bayeux Tapestry and other such internationally renowned arenas. To be known as "The House of Manannan" it will offer visitors of all ages a unique insight into the history of the Island.

There have been numerous periods of importance in Peel's history, many of which have played a roll in the development of the Island's nation-hood. The Viking settlement of the area was one such period and excavations have uncovered important burial sites. One site revealed the remains of a female subsequently known as "The Pagan Lady". The grave was unusual in that it was a curious mixture of Christian and Pagan rituals. A very fine bead necklace was recovered from the

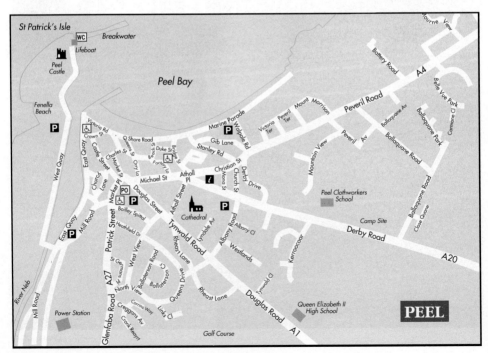

grave and you can see the real thing in the Museum at Douglas.

Very important prisoners have been incarcerated in Peel Castle over the ages and the Bard himself, William Shakespeare, makes mention in Henry VI of one famous detainee, Eleanor – Duchess of Gloucester. For fourteen long and difficult years the Cathedral crypt was the prison of the Duchess, who was accused of treason and sorcery against Henry VI as she sought to advance her husband's claim to the throne of England. Her fellow plotters were not to taste the "joys" of Manx prison life as Roger Bolingbroke was executed and Margery Joudemain, the Witch of Eye, was burnt to death. History records that the Duchess was a difficult prisoner, who had to be carefully guarded against escape or even suicide. If such a wealthy and perhaps arrogant woman could be held against her will in conditions of great deprivation, it is not a wonder that her ghost is said to haunt the crypt.

Once bitten by the Peel bug, most people park their vehicles and walk everywhere, but just in case you are visiting or staying here and are without transport, the aptly named Empire Garage can take care of your transport requirements. No problem in finding them, just wander along the Promenade taking in the august, almost imperial looking coastline extending away northwards. The amiable staff will soon fix you up with a suitable car to extend your Island exploration.

The narrow streets of Peel with their sandstone built cottages and houses act as a wonderful backdrop to the bay. The purpose of many of the buildings has changed and guessing their former use is a fascinating way of enjoying a walk around the city. The shops offer a variety of goods and although lacking any of the big national superstores, they do give a very personal service. Hobbies are catered for in Michael Street, where Hanneke's Handicrafts are able to fulfil your needlework requirements. If your forte is painting then the friendly Dutch lady can advise you on painting eggs right through the spectrum to glass decorative, and she operates a mail order service.

Education has always been valued by the people of the West and Philip Christian, a native born son of the city who died in 1655, left money

View from Peel Castle

Peel

to educate the poorest boys and girls of Peel. Moving towards more modern times there have been Latin, Navigation, English and Mathematical schools in Peel and there is now a very fine High School, opened a few years ago by Her Majesty the Queen, in whose honour it is named.

One of Peel's greatest exports has been its people and with a strong tradition of seamanship behind them, it is small wonder that the sons and daughters of what must be the smallest city in the British Isles have spread out all over the world. George Cannon was born in Michael Street on the 3rd December 1794. Some thirty one years later he married Ann Quayle, a girl from round the corner in Douglas Street. After becoming converts to the Mormon faith, they emigrated along with thousands of others to the USA. Departing from

Liverpool on 3rd September 1842 on the sailing ship *"Sydney"*, the voyage was to be one of tragedy for the family as, forty one days out, the cold waters of the Atlantic received the body of Ann Quayle. Two years after leaving Liverpool to seek religious freedom, both parents had died but their memory lives on in the hearts of some twenty thousand direct descendants, many of them leaders in their own fields of work becoming Congressmen, Senators, Chief Justices, Federal Judges and much more. On your walk round Peel have a look at number 25 Douglas Street ... that's where Ann Quayle lived.

Obviously during the course of your wanderings the pangs of thirst and hunger may well strike. Peel has a variety of pubs – Creg Malin, the Royal – hotels, snack bars and cafes, each reflecting their own style. Sport is important in Peel and there are occasions when sand racing attracts thousands of people to the seafront. Golf is popular and the eighteen hole course presents a real challenge.

There are a number of small hotels, guesthouses and self-catering establishments in and close by Peel to suit all tastes. The forward

Island Photographic

Peel

thinking City Fathers have recognised the value of providing a campsite and have invested a six figure sum in Peel Camping Park. Situated on the edge of town, a modern amenity block, electric hook up points and other facilities offer an excellent situation.

Public Amenities
Harbour Master's Office (01624) 842338
Peel Commissioners (Town Hall) (01624) 842341
Peel Post Office (01624) 842282
Police Station (not continuously manned) (01624) 842208, (01624) 631212

Banks
Barclays, Michael Street (Central Switchboard) (01624) 682000
Isle of Man Bank, Atholl Street (01624) 842122
Lloyds, Douglas Street (01624) 638000

Tourist Information
Peel Commissioners (Town Hall) (01624) 842341
Peel Bus Depot (01624) 842349

St John's

Inland and to the East of Peel is St John's. Dotted about the Guide are various references to the politically important role that this pretty village has played and continues to play to this very day in the life of the Isle of Man. Sitting comfortably with an air of elegance, hugging the gap between *Slieau Whallian* and *Beary Mountain* – traced back to the Scandinavian for Farm of the Shieling – it is well worth a visit. Every 5th July, all roads lead to St John's. On this our National Day the Island celebrates over a thousand years of unbroken government by holding the traditional open air Tynwald. Thousand upon thousands of Islanders and visitors make the journey to watch the ancient ceremony. The laws of Mann which have been enacted during the last year are proclaimed in Manx and English, in summarised form, by the Deemsters – Manx equivalent to the British High Court Judges – to the gathered public, after which Tynwald has a formal meeting within the Royal Chapel of St John's. Sitting at a lofty height above the throngs

73

Tynwald Hill, St John's

and on the summit of Tynwald Hill is the Lieutenant Governor. Below him and arranged in descending order are variously the Keys, Legislative Council, Crown Officers, Churchmen, Heads of Local Authorities, Captains of the Parishes and the six Coroners of the Island. The formal part of the day is supported by a Fair and a good time is had by all!

One of the most popular developments of recent years has seen the site of the old Tynwald Woollen Mills change from just the production of fine woollen garments into a full blown craft and shopping centre. A special mention must be made here of Roly's Chocolates. This small shop turns out hand made exquisite chocolates using the finest materials from Belgium. Roly's are able to design chocolates to a customer's own requirements, and a visit to the Tynwald Craft Centre would not be complete without calling into this lovely shop.

There is plenty of parking at the complex and it is on the bus routes and coach tour itineraries. Children are catered for with play areas and there are excellent catering facilities. A visit is highly recommended.

Kirk Michael

Now using the shortened version of its name, it was previously known as Kirk Michael Towne or Michaeltown. Fame comes to this sunny village at least twice a year as the racing motorcycles flash through the main road at incredible mind-boggling speeds. TT mythology tells that the inhabitants of Kirk Michael have the flattest feet in the Isle of Man by reason of the houses edging right up to the race course ... the writer doesn't think it is true, but the inhabitants do put up with the road closures in a very gracious manner. A good place from which to watch the racing is the Mitre. There are some interesting shops spaced out along the main road.

Glen Wyllin, sometimes spelt without a break between the words, meaning Mill Glen, was once a famous tourist attraction much helped by the railway. Nothing remains of the railway now except two lonely sandstone support pillars for the old bridge which they used to carry the line high above the Glen. None of the beauty has been lost however and happy days can still be had down on the beach, and there are plenty of pleasant walks in the neighbourhood.

Churchyards, as with all burial grounds, are the providers of a potted history of bygone days and Kirk Michael's is no exception. Within these hallowed grounds are buried five bishops. There is

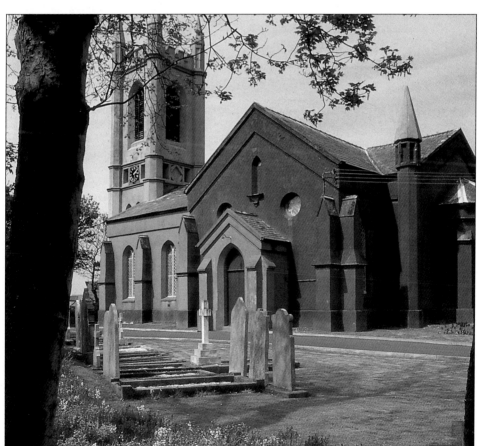

Kirk Michael Church

a memorial stone to that much loved priest, "The Good" Bishop Wilson. This kind and generous hearted man did much for the people of Ellan Vannin in his long and beneficial stewardship of the Christian faith. It is reputed that prior to his death an elm tree was cut down to provide the wood for his coffin. Bishop Wilson planted that tree when he first arrived on the Island to take up this great office, some fifty seven years earlier.

Ballaugh

The Parish from which the village takes its name measures some five miles in a North to South line and about three miles from East to West. The boundaries touch Jurby to the North, Michael and Lezayre to the South and East. It is the beginning of the scenery that is so typical of this corner of the Island where the lonely glens run down to the low sandy cliffs of the shore against a background of the northern mountains and hills. The modern village is some way from the sea, straddling the main Peel to Ramsey road and you can clearly see the new church – built 1832 – from afar. Approximately a mile and a half nearer the sea lies old Kirk Ballaugh Church with its very distinctive "leaning" gate posts. Parish Registers are still an important source of information and Ballaugh has the oldest in the Island dating from 1598. If you visit this consecrated place, look at the bog oak notice board enumerating the rectors back to the earliest days of the fifteenth century.

Jurby, Andreas & Bride

These, the three northern most Parishes fall within the Sheadings of Michael and Ayre respectively. They share virtually the same scenery and the only high ground in the area is found in the shape of the Bride Hills. Very much farming country, the northern plain is a maze of roads and lanes zigzagging between the villages. Although well signposted, it is easy to get lost but a quick look over your shoulder towards the mountains will soon put you back on course.

Jurby in more modern times grew up around the old Air Force base and, although now closed, good use is being made of the site with various small businesses based there. A visit to the old garrison church is worth a diversion and if you have time, wander through the churchyard. There is a lot of history to be imagined by reading the inscriptions on the old headstones and the church porch has a fine collection of stone crosses. In the new part of the churchyard, the well kept graves of the Polish, Canadian, Anzac and British airmen who made the ultimate sacrifice, are laid out in neat rows. On a clear day, stand at the back of the church. The Mull of Galloway and its lighthouse seem almost as if they could be touched and if you listen carefully ... you can hear the silence! There are times when even the tranquillity of Jurby is shattered but that is only on the occasions when the motor racing enthusiasts operate one of their sporting events on the old air strip. The Gliding Club offers the only clue to the aeronautical past the area enjoyed and apart from them and the yearly air show, the airfield is virtually unused for flying.

Andreas has always been a pleasant village much enjoying its peaceful rural existence, largely uninterrupted since the end of the Viking era. In the 1940s, the land to the North and East of the village was utilised as an RAF base and the villagers became used to great flying machines overhead at all times of day and night. Roads and lanes which had previously only been wide enough to suit a

Old Ballaugh Church

horse and cart were enlarged, and it was not an unusual sight to see large aircraft being manoeuvred about on the roads skirting the edge of this ancient village. The heady days of the wartime emergency over, Andreas quickly reverted to its placid ways. That was until 1995 when the old airfields of Andreas and Jurby were used as backdrops for a film called the Brylcream Boys, look out for it at your nearest cinema – it will give you a good idea about the Island's scenery.

For the lover of architecture the Parish Church of Kirk Andreas with its Lombardic campanile is unexpected, but the Italian style sits well and at ease in the Manx countryside. It was built in 1802 to replace a church from the thirteenth century, the time when parishes were first formed on the Island. There was great excitement in 1869 when Anglo-Saxon coins were discovered during the building of the bell tower. Dedicated to St Andrew, probably during the period of Scottish Rule circa 1275 to 1334, there are indications that suggest a much earlier church, whose name has been lost, occupied the site. During the Second World War the spire was removed from the church to give a clear flight path for the planes using RAF Jurby and RAF Andreas. The Andreas carved stones are very fine examples of the craftsmanship of those far off days and one, a pillar, is particularly interesting with its inscription in Roman capitals and letters from the Ogham alphabet. Such carvings were seldom found outside of Wales. The Grosvenor Hotel in the centre of the village is the northernmost public house in the Island and when you have finished your explorations and need refreshment, pay them a visit, you will not be disappointed.

Sitting on the slopes of the Bride Hills, the village of Bride seems almost becalmed in a haven of peace. It has known troubled times though, and its earlier history can best be described as turbulent. Frequently the victims of raids by pirates and marauders, the poor inhabitants often went in fear of their very lives. There is a Manx ballad which gives the origins of the old tradition that the people of Kirk Bride always used to eat their meat course before the soup. On clear summer days the smoke from the Bride chimneys could be seen from the Galloway coast and the story is told that

Jurby Church

the villainous chieftain Cutlar MacCulloch and his men would, on seeing this, set sail for a good Manx feed. On one occasion arriving at a wedding feast just after soup had been taken, they devoured the meat prepared for the guests. The incident is celebrated in verse form.

The rovers were many, the wedding guests few,
So the rovers sat down to the mutton and stew,
But from that day to this, as our North custom tells,
We trust neither to wind, nor to mermaid spells,
But first of all eat – our coveted meat,
And over the broth tell of MacCulloch's feat.

Marked clearly on the map to the West of Bride is Thurot Cottage, a private house whose building was made possible by utilising timbers from the defeated French Men of War lead by the "Bellisle", under the command of Captain Thurot. This battle was witnessed by Bishop Hildesley in February 1760 and would in all likelihood have been seen and certainly heard from Bride. The church at Bride as with many other of our religious buildings is a working record of the past and the Celtic Crosses are worth a visit. There is a car park beside the road below the church and there are a number of pleasant walks to be enjoyed in the neighbourhood. The village was honoured in 1995 by having a new rose named after it.

The taste that's stood the test of time

Traditionally brewed in Douglas, Isle of Man since 1850,
Okell's Best Bitter contains no ingredient or preparation whatsoever
as a substitute for pure malt, sugar or hops.

Ramsey

Distances Ballasalla 24, Castletown 26, Douglas 16, Laxey 8, Peel 16, Port Erin 28, Port St Mary 28.

The Chronicles of Mann in about 1250 have the northern town recorded as *Ramsa* seemingly drawn from the old Scandinavian language. In the Manorial Roll of 1703 the current and English spelling of the name is indicated. The Manx Gaelic has it as *Ramsaa* which on closer inspection is similar to Ramsa, the Scandinavian for Wild Garlic River. Old OS maps however show the river as *Stroon ny Craue*, Manx for The Stream of the Wild Garlic.

There are no buildings of great antiquity in Ramsey save for old Ballure Church. The Burial Register dates from 1611 and the building was reported in 1637 to be in a near ruinous state, but over the years at various times it has been restored. Bishop Wilson held a thanksgiving service here to celebrate deliverance from the French and to honour Commodore Elliot's victory. Ramsey in the last decade or so has been trying to decide whether to go for a totally modern style of rebuild or aim for a blend of the old with the new. In fact it is probably towards the latter they are drifting and there is a happy mingling of architectural styles, particularly on the sea front.

Presumably the reason for much of Ramsey's lack of old buildings lies in the fact that it was the site of much destruction across the centuries. Olaf, King of Mann, was murdered by his nephew Reginald near the harbour in 1154. Somerled, the twelfth century Thane of Argyll, made a historic landing here, and Robert the Bruce a century later passed through on his way to besiege Castle Rushen. The prestigious prefix to the name must have been hard earned and it most likely evolved from the fact that Ramsey was the gateway of kings long before the coming of Godred Crovan in 1079. Landing in Ramsey became a lot easier when the magnificent Ramsey Pier was built. Thrusting itself out into deep water it quickly became a popular stopping off point for the steamers en route to other ports of call. At the present it is closed for repairs and the future hopefully will be one that ensures its well being.

Situated at the mouth of the Sulby River, Ramsey was undoubtedly an island. In 1630 the

Ramsey

RAMSEY

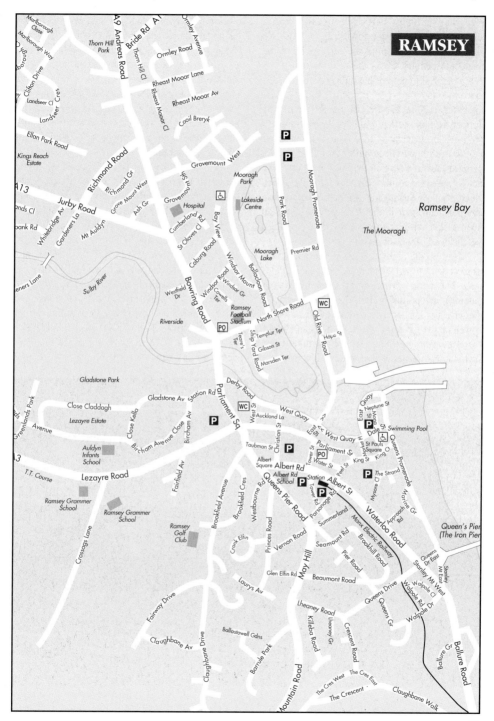

Ramsey Bay

The Mooragh

town was virtually destroyed by the sea, a continuous threat that the townsfolk were to live with and suffer from, until the early years of the nineteenth century. From the re-direction of the river and the silting up of the old harbour entrance, good was to come. As a result, Ramsey now possesses the enchanting Mooragh Park. The harbour is pure joy for anyone even remotely interested in water activities. Across the harbour the Ramsey shipyard has built many fine vessels, the most famous of which the *"Star of India"* is a famous attraction in the American port city of San Diego. Ramsey's shipyard can also claim to have played a major part in the development of the oil business by building the world's first two ships specifically designed as oil tankers.

Many people are now finding their way to the sunniest part of the Island and using it as a holiday base. The pace of life on the Isle of Man is generally much slower than that of the adjacent isles and it is fair to say that Ramsey's way of life is even more relaxed than the rest of Ellan Vannin. There is much to do and see in this market town. Shopping is effortless and if you are like everyone else on holiday, you tend to window shop before taking the plunge and purchasing holiday presents. If you are worried about carrying presents home ask if the shop can mail them for you, some of the shops offer this service. Eating out is not difficult in the capital of the North, most of the pubs and hotels offer bar meals and Okell's have the Central, Plough, Royal George, Stanley and the Britannia here. For the younger element the Nightlife Club offers a style to suit.

Moving in or out of Ramsey is easy by public transport but please note the electric trams operate a reduced service during the winter. For the self-contained traveller Iris House in Albert Square is situated close to most of Ramsey's amenities. A good base for specialist holidays such as sailing, fishing, walking, golf, bird watching or indeed just for relaxing in. Railway enthusiasts will find it particularly convenient.

Before leaving Ramsey and its environs, it is worth pointing out that if your leaning is towards an action type of holiday, the Venture Centre at Lewaigue Farm, Maughold, could provide the outlet for any surplus energy. The Venture Centre

Ramsey

is the Island's premier outdoor centre providing a wide range of adventure activities for the more agile visitor. Activities include archery, abseiling, air rifle shooting, assault course, canoeing, climbing, clay pigeon shooting, grass skiing and sailing. They offer full residential courses for both children and adults; half and full day activities are available for visitors staying elsewhere on the Island. Activities for one to one hundred persons can be provided and there are substantial group discounts. Getting to the Venture Centre is easy by car or you can use the Manx Electric Railway, they have a halt close by.

A little way to the West of Ramsey lies without doubt one of the finest houses in the Isle of Man. Home of Fred and Di Parkes, Kerrowmoar House, a magnificent Georgian House set in mature grounds in the midst of some of the Island's most productive farmland guarantees by its very seclusion tranquillity from the moment visitors arrive. Guests have complete access to the paddocks with tame sheep and horses, sun patio, a heated indoor swimming pool, an all-weather tennis court and an almost limitless choice of hill and country walks after which they can relax in front of a log fire. Mentioned in the Manorial Roll of 1703 as Great Quarterland, the traditions epitomised by Kerrowmoar allow this family home to offer get away from it all holidays with superb freshly cooked food and service in the best of the old country styles. Discovered by Country Living magazine and the Daily Express, Kerrowmoar has been honoured with an invitation to join the "Best Loved Hotels of the World" Directory. Worthy ambassadors for the Island, no praise is too high for this very fine establishment.

Public Amenities
Harbour Master's Office (01624) 812245
Police Station (01624) 812234
Ramsey Cottage Hospital (01624) 813254
Ramsey Town Commissioners (Town Hall) (01624) 812228
Ramsey Post Office, Gladstone Park (01624) 816735, Ramsey Court Row Post Office (01624) 812248

Banks
Barclays, Parliament Street (01624) 813124
Isle of Man Bank, Parliament Street (01624) 812829
Lloyds, Parliament Street (01624) 638000
Midland, St Paul's Square (01624) 684851
TSB Bank, Parliament Street (01624) 813596

Building Societies
Britannia (IOM), Market Square (01624) 816733

Leisure Centres
The Ventre Centre (Maughold) (01624) 814240
Mooragh Park (01624) 813375
Ramsey Swimming Pool, Queens Promenade (01624) 812852

Tourist Information
Ramsey Bus Depot (01624) 812151
Ramsey Electric Railway Station (Seasonal) (01624) 812249

Laxey

Laxey

Distances Ballasalla 17, Castletown 20, Douglas 8, Peel 19, Port Erin 23, Port St Mary 24, Ramsey 8.

Salmon River was the name given by the early Scandinavian visitors to this area. Translated as Laxey as we now know it, the village has represented the Island on so many magazine covers, brochures, photographs, newspaper articles, radio and television programmes that it has become as synonymous with the Isle of Man as our famous kippers or the TT Races. Built up over the centuries Laxey sprawls along the sides of a deep glen, running down from the mine workings in its upper reaches, to the tiny harbour at the North end of a wide bay.

Old papers of village life record that in the eighteenth century large shipments of fish were sent from the port, to Sicily. In present times the main products are flour, still manufactured on the site of the 1513 mill, woollen goods and the famous Meerschaum and Briar pipes. Laxey Pipes on the Quay warmly welcome visitors to their factory and if you decide to treat yourself to a new pipe there are fifteen styles and six finishes to the Meerschaum to choose from. If you are a DIY enthusiast why not treat yourself to a pipe carving kit. The biggest industry Laxey has ever had was the mines. Lead, copper, zinc and silver were wrenched from the cold, wet and dank ground. Highly profitable in their heyday, between the years 1876 to 1882 the Great Laxey Mines paid out the highest total in dividends of all their competitor lead mines in the British Isles. Earnings of this magnitude ensured a reasonable standard of living for the inhabitants. Now the village is a very pleasant place to live and it has seen considerable expansion in recent times.

One piece of past glory that remains unchanged is the "Lady Isabella". Standing aloof from the purpose for which it was originally designed the biggest working water wheel in the world still performs its functions, much as it did from the first day of operation back in 1854. Named after the Governor of the day's wife, it is a stark reminder of the hard work that went into winning Laxey's wealth, pumping water from as much as two thousand feet below ground. The dimensions of the wheel are formidable with a circumference of 227 feet and ninety five steps lifting you up to the platform 75 feet from the ground. Can you imagine ending your shift at the bottom of the mine and climbing up ladders, one hundred feet in length to the surface. Little wonder the mine owners didn't object when the men requested permission to work "double shifts". Manx National Heritage have done an excellent job of interpreting life as it was in the mines and the mine trail is a must for every visitor. On a fine day take a picnic and enjoy the sense of the past.

The voluntary organisation Laxey Heritage Trust can be found in the old Fire Station on the road just before the Wheel. It is a treasure house of information and the delightful people who man it on a part time basis are real enthusiasts for the village and area. There are lots of good walking trails to enjoy and it may not be a bad idea to check with the folk at the Heritage Trust.

Perched high above Laxey and just along the *Ballaragh Road* from King Orry's Grave lie Ballachrink Farm Cottages; *Ballachrink* translates into English as Hill Farm. The real meaning of Ballaragh has been lost but it is likely that it was derived from *Balley-arraght*, meaning farm of the spectre or apparition, in fact nowadays the only spectre visible is the vision provided by the beautiful views from Ballachrink of the hills and coastline. There is an atmospheric feel to the cottages and the sympathetic way in which they blend into the countryside, coupled with the luxurious standards set by Kate and Peter have thrust these delightful buildings right to the top of the Isle of Man's self-catering sector. Guests want for nothing and it is recommended to book early to avoid disappointment.

Lower down the Glen there are plenty of activities for young and old with gardens and the beach for the children to enjoy, whilst the older tourist can take in the small folk museum near the station or use the time to take a trip up Snaefell. Hunger is a subject you need never experience in Laxey. There are a number of eating houses and pubs that will keep you going,

Lady Isabella

just keep an eye open for the Okell's Falcon, the sign of good food, wines and ales.

Public Amenities
Harbour Master's Office (01624) 861663
Laxey Commissioners (Town Hall) (01624) 861241
Laxey Post Office (01624) 861209
Police Station (not continuously manned) (01624) 861210, (01624) 631212

Banks
Isle of Man Bank, New Road (01624) 626232

Tourist Information
Electric Railway Station (Seasonal) (01624) 861226
Electric Railway Sub-Station (01624) 861244
Laxey Heritage Trust, Mines Road (01624) 862007
Restricted hours – summer only)

Onchan

The patron saint of the Parish of Onchan was St Christopher, better known by his Gaelic name of *Conchenn*, meaning Dog-Head or Wolf-Head. There is a strong case to be argued that the name of the village is identified with St Connachan, who was Bishop of Sodor and Man in 540 AD. Remarkably within the porch of St Peter's Church there are three cross slabs which depict dog-like monsters. The present church built in 1833 has no particular style of architecture but within the churchyard there are many interesting graves amongst them being that of Lieutenant Edward Reeves RN, one of Nelson's officers who fought with him at Trafalgar. The earlier church on this site witnessed the marriage of Captain Bligh of "Bounty" fame to a Manx girl, Elizabeth Betham, daughter of the Collector of Customs on the Island. Bligh was reputed to have rued the day that he came to the Isle of Man and met up with Fletcher Christian. Although the Church Register is not the oldest on the Island, it does date back to 1627 and perusal of the list of vicars commences with one appointed in 1408.

In Church Road at the place known as "The Butt" there is a quaint building with a carved head over the door. Known as Molly Caroon's cottage it was formerly used as a mission hall. Now restored it is occasionally opened to the public so that they may sample a taste of Manx tradition. Close by the cottage the Manx Nature Conservation Trust have an Urban Reserve; this wet-lands project is easily accessible to the public and although not a large site, it is well worth a visit. The old part of the village is grouped around the church, but with Onchan expanding so rapidly in recent years, with a number of large estates spread around the hilly countryside, the village has the second largest centre of population on the Island. A fairly new landmark is the King Edward Bay clubhouse serving a challenging and very demanding golf course laid out on the hilly terrain of Banks Howe. Near the centre of the village is Onchan Park where you can enjoy boating, tennis, bowls, pitch'n put golf, or the frequent stock car races.

If the country life is your choice, then consider Hillberry Manor. Sitting proudly on the edge of Onchan it is a veritable oasis of peace and tranquillity and the cuisine has few challengers for its variety and excellence. A real "get away from it all" establishment run by the nicest of people (See page 32 for advert).

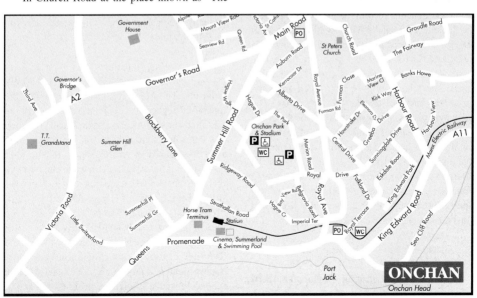

The Coasts and Islands of the Isle of Man

Coasts

The Chasms

Mythology informs us that the Isle of Man came into being as the result of an argument between two warriors, one in Ireland, Finn MacCoole, and one of unknown name in the adjacent island of England. During the course of their dispute a large lump of Ireland was hurled from the vicinity of Lough Neagh and missing its intended target landed in the middle of the North Irish Sea and that's how the Isle of Man arrived!

The sea has always played an integral part in the development of the Island and it is no surprise that the coastline still ranks importantly in our lives. Stand anywhere on the sea's edge and look at the views. To the East there rises the impressive bulk of the Cumbrian mountains and the English Lake District, to the North are the purple headed hills of Galloway in Scotland, over to the West lie Ulster's Mountains of Mourne, to the South West the Republic of Ireland's Wicklow Mountains loom above the horizon,while to the South is Snowdonia in Wales, clearly seen on a fine day. With five countries as neighbours, it is a wonder that this small Island has remained segregated from the hustle and bustle of modern life for so long. The seemingly endless changing contours of the cliffs, crowded into such a small land mass leaves no room for boredom. Indeed it is difficult to imagine where else in the British Islands you could be offered such a wide variety of coastal scenery. From the steep wave-lashed cliffs of the East and South to the long sandy cliffs of the North and West there is choice for everyone.

Douglas to Spanish Head

From Douglas heading South, the cliffs gradually diminish in height all the way down to *Poyll Vaaish* to the West of Castletown. On past the low-lying shores of *Bay ny Carrickey* the cliffs from Port St Mary to the Sound seem suddenly to rear up from the deepwaters surrounding the Mull Peninsula. The Manx National Trust area to the South of Cregneash Village boasts some of the most dramatic cliff scenery on the Island. Tradition says that some great upheaval in the earth's crust aeons ago stacked up great blocks of rock to form the Chasms. Modern science indicates that a more likely explanation is that their incredible shape was formed by the action of wind and waves down through the centuries. Warning, there are deep holes in the Chasms often hidden beneath your feet by clumps of springy heather. Please take care and keep tight control of any children in your party. Spanish Head is a promontory associated with the Spanish Armada. Folklore informs us that a galleon was wrecked here as the English navy chased the survivors of that great event down through the Irish Sea. It would be doubtful if anyone got ashore from such an incident.

The Sound to Peel

The cliffs from the Sound to Port Erin are as rugged as those on the East side of the peninsula. The sheer drops into the sea leave no room for complacency and great care must be exercised when walking in this area. If you are crossing the edge of Bay Fine, look down – you may be lucky and see Basking sharks close in on the coast, sometimes it helps to wear a pair of sunglasses to see them.

Perched spectacularly on Port Erin's Bradda Head is Milner's Tower. The tower can be reached by following the pretty coastal footpath from Bradda Glen or by driving part of the way up a minor road from Bradda West. Although the permanent coastguard look-outpost is no longer, the Isle of Man's own Coastguard Service do keep watch from the Head in certain bad weather conditions. The views from the top of the tower are second to none and there is a plaque indicating the position from which a world prize-winning

photograph was taken in 1936. Built in 1871 as a memorial to William Milner, the head of a firm of Liverpool safe manufacturers, it is formed in the shape of the barrel of a lock, with the inner end uppermost.

Port Erin to *Gob yn Ushtey*, Point of Water or Waterfall, has the highest cliffs on the Isle of Man rising in places over a thousand feet out of the water. The cliffs here act as a huge windbreak, affording protection from the strong westerlys, to the farms to the East. *Cronk ny Arrey Laa* dwarfs even the grandeur of Spanish Head as it tumbles precipitously 1,500 feet to the sea. Stretching away northwards the cliffs dip down to Niarbyl and then gradually rise up, past and beyond Glen Maye, peaking at Contrary Head, before plunging down almost to sea level at Peel Castle. Interestingly Contrary Head, it is said, was named from the fact that the SE-going and NW-going tidal streams divide and meet off this headland.

Peel like Port Erin has its own tower looking down on it from a height. Standing on the summit of Corrin's Hill, it is believed that the remains of a Quaker and his family are buried here. A few yards from Corrin's Tower is a sacred place, much revered by the early Christians, St Patrick's Well. Tradition has it that when St Patrick landed there,

Looking South over Peel

the horse he was riding shed one of its silver shoes and on that very spot a spring of water gushed from the rock and formed a well. The pathway to Corrin's Memorial gently threads its way through the lush green turf and when in season, the heather, bracken and gorse that does so much to brighten the hillside.

Peel to Cranstal

From the Stack, the Point to the North end of Peel Bay, the coastline changes from sandstone cliffs to high sandy headlands. Mother nature has been busy here and in severe weather large sections of the coast have been washed away. Kirk Michael to Blue Point is a coast of moderately high sandy cliffs changing to fine sanded dunes. The Ayres really have no cliffs. The sea laps the very edge of the flat plains and it is not until Cranstal is reached that any height is gained by the coast.

Ramsey to Onchan

With sandy cliffs bordering the northern end of Ramsey Bay the coastline of Mann suddenly breaks back into ruggedness, with the massive headland of Maughold looming out of the crystal clear waters beyond Ramsey's southern flank. Rounding the vertical walls of Maughold Head and its fine lighthouse, the cliffs plunge down to Port Mooar and then rise ever upwards until their high point, in the vicinity of Dhoon Bay. Laxey is tucked into the mouth of the Great Glen, protected by Laxey Head to the North and from the southerly winds by the bulk of Clay Head. On past Clay Head, an example of the Anglicisation of the Manx language but admittedly so much easier to pronounce than *Kione ny Cleigh*, lies Groudle. This part of the parish of Onchan owes its origins to the Scandinavian word *Krappdalr*, Narrow Glen. At the North end of Douglas Bay lies Port Jack. Tradition has it that it got its name from the mate of a small ship feeling its way South along the coast in foggy weather. Perhaps it was the sound of the breakers on the shore that made him call out "Port Jack, Port Jack" and the Captain duly obliged and headed out to sea again.

Islands

The Calf of Man

The Isle of Man has only one real satellite island although there are a number of small islets. Being an island race we are very possessive of our country and anything that rises even a few feet above sea level is claimed and if possible nominated for island status. The main island is the Calf of Man. In the ownership of the Manx National Trust it is possible to visit the Calf during the summer months. If you don't have your own boat, regular sailings operate from Port Erin and occasionally from Port St Mary.

Should you be using your own boat, take care, the waters surrounding the Calf are dangerous and should be treated with the greatest of respect. Do not go too close to the shoreline, several drying rocks project from the base of the cliffs and the coast is foul to a distance of 2 cables (for the landlubbers that is about 185 metres or 608 feet) offshore. There are two harbours or to be more specific two landing places on the Calf. South Haven which is a small inlet close to the East of *The Burroo*, Dome-shaped Hill – the name of the nearby large rock – and Grants Harbour, little more than a cleft in the rocks on the North East corner.

The Calf has a circumference of five miles and a land mass of about 1,000 acres and is now a bird sanctuary of international repute. There is a long history to the Island but it seems as if it never had a large population, a legacy perhaps of the strong currents that flow around its shores and the difficult landing conditions. A Celtic stone cross of great antiquarian value was discovered there many years ago which is believed to have been from a long since lost ancient keeill. The cross can be seen in the Manx Museum. In the dangerous years of the English Civil War, *Yn Stanlagh Mooar* fortified the Calf, for a rental to the owner of 500 puffins a year. The only crofting now done on the Calf is sheep farming and there is a fine flock of Loaghtan sheep roaming freely about the Island.

The cliffs and wide expanses of springy turf

Point of Ayre

and heather are nesting grounds to a colossal variety of bird life and the Island is well populated by rabbits. Walking can be hazardous with thousands of rabbit holes penetrating the ground. Brer Rabbit must have been the main source of food there, for a story is told about an inhabitant who not only used them for food but also as payment for his rent, and who became so fed up with his diet that he composed a prayer known as the "Calf of Man Grace".

For rabbits hot, and rabbits cold,
For rabbits young, and rabbits old,
For rabbits tender, rabbits tough,
I thank the Lord, I've had enough.

The Chicken Rock

Off the South West corner of the Calf is a small islet called the Chicken Rock. The rock is named from the once numerous Mother Carey's Chickens, a seabird which frequents the waters of the area. Standing sentinel over a dangerous reef is a tall granite lighthouse. Built in 1875 to replace two earlier lighthouses on the Calf, this guardian of shipping is now un-manned and fully automated as a consequence of a fire in 1964, from which the keepers were lucky to escape with their lives.

Kitterland

The sea passage between the Calf of Man and the Isle of Man is divided into two channels by a small island called *Kitterland*. The derivation of this name is shrouded in the mists of the past. There is an argument that the name comes from the Scandinavian word, the latter part of which means island, with the first part being either a personal name or kid's (as in goat). Probably the more romantic and more acceptable definition of the name is from the great Baron Kitter who was wrecked there in the days of Olaf. In 1852 the brig *"Lily"* was wrecked on Kitterland and subsequently exploded killing all the salvars, save one. It ranks as one of the worst shipping disasters to befall the Isle of Man. There is a monument to the victims in Rushen churchyard.

Niarbyl

The mariner sailing up the West coast searching for islands to shelter behind in stormy weather will be disappointed. Between Port Erin and Peel there is but one place which could even be remotely described as an island. Lying below Elby Point at Niarbyl is a rock which is much frequented by sea anglers and it is certain that little more than a coracle would find safety there. The disappointed mariner soon cheers up however when he reaches the fishing port of Peel.

St Patrick's Isle

Built around the estuary of the River Neb, Peel's outer boundaries are protected by the imposing Peel Castle, sitting astride St Patrick's Isle. Now no longer technically an island, St Patrick's Isle is joined to the Manx mainland by a causeway. Bridging Fenella's Beach, the causeway takes the visitor onto an island whose fascinating history is possibly unequalled by anywhere else in the known world. Within its five acres, almost every period of architecture from prehistoric earthworks to the fortifications erected during the Napoleonic wars is represented. It witnessed the early struggles of Christian missionaries against the Pagans. At various troubled times down through the ages it has been a garrison, an armoury and a place of retreat. In the past it has been used as an ecclesiastical prison and there are believed to be no less than eight bishops buried there. As an interesting footnote, Bishop Wilson in 1725 was in dispute with Lieutenant Governor Thomas Horton, over the latter's plan to remove the roof remains from the Island's St Germain's Cathedral and use them in the building of new stables at Castletown. It seems that the vessel used to carry away the Cathedral's roof timbers was lost on its subsequent voyage. A place to whet the appetite of anyone with even the slightest of interest in the past!

Conister Rock

Coasting northwards round the Point of Ayre the mariner finds a shoreline devoid of islands until Douglas Bay is reached. Everyone who makes their landfall in Douglas cannot help but be impressed by the picturesque building that graces Conister or St Mary's Rock. Known as the Tower of Refuge, it was built by Sir William and Lady Hillary in 1832 as a refuge to shelter the shipwrecked sailors from vessels that had been driven by gales and storms onto these jagged and dangerous rocks. It acted as the spur to Sir William and he went on to become the founder of the Royal National Lifeboat Institution – the RNLI.

St Michael's Isle

To complete the tour of Manxland's islands the journey will take you to St Michael's Island. Lying just off the North East point of the Langness Peninsula, it is joined to the mainland by a stone built causeway. Looking at the map it almost seems as if the promontory is boot shaped with St Michael's Island forming the heel. Often known as Fort Island ... what historical events this small island must have witnessed. The Island guards Derbyhaven from the worst excesses of East and South East gales and as such was well used by the Vikings and others to shelter their boats. The remains of the only buildings standing on the island are of a round, stone built fort and a chapel. Built in the seventeenth century the fort is in very good condition and has a date, 1645 inscribed on a stone above the gateway. The Seventh Earl of Derby, *Yn Stanlagh Mooar* must have feared for his Kingdom to erect this fortification. Remains of earth embankments are still clearly visible on the Island and it is thought that they may have been raised at the time of Magnus's landing here in 1250. The ruined chapel probably stands on the site of an ancient keeill and a close inspection of the building reveals alterations to its dimensions at different times.

A local story tells of a much loved priest who was famous amongst the inhabitants for his teachings and kind heart, and who proposed that a new church should be built on St Michael's Isle. The idea of this twelfth or early thirteenth century church had come to him in a vision during which St Michael pointed out to the priest the location of the building and a finely designed altar within.

Working with a will the people gave their labour freely and had soon finished the church. There was however no way that their meagre resources could provide the fine altar seen in the vision ... that was, until the confession of a dying shipwrecked pirate revealed a horde of gold buried in the churchyard. At first hesitant to heed the dying pirate's encouragement to use it for the good of the people, the priest refused. Eventually convinced that there was no one left alive to whom the treasure could belong, this kindly man of God bought a statue of the Madonna and around the neck hung a string of pearls found with the treasure trove.

One day a vessel came to an anchor in Derbyhaven and two of the crew came ashore, begging the priest to come out to their vessel and minister to one of their colleagues. Suspecting nothing, he went with them. Alas it was another pirate ship, a sister to the one from which the dying pirate had been saved; they had come in search of their treasure. The next morning the villagers found the church had been sacked and their priest murdered by the very pearls from around the statue's neck. To this very day it is believed that whoever strikes the walls of this ancient building will hear the moans of the saintly victim, accompanied by the jingle of coins.

The Raglan Pier - Port Erin

Mountains, Valleys, Glens and Parks

Mountains

Mountains in whatever country you are visiting have a mystique of their own. They draw your eyes ever skyward, almost enticing you to climb them.

What they also guarantee, especially in the northern hemisphere are large areas of unspoilt countryside. The Isle of Man is no exception to the rule with some 40% of its land mass uninhabited. There are twenty five peaks over 1,000 feet in height and many of them are well over 1,500 feet above sea level. The Manx mountains have a finely sculptured appearance almost as if they have been moulded by a giant artist. Snaefell has pride of place as Ellan Vannin's highest peak. You can never tire of looking at it from most places on the Island and it is home to the finest electric mountain railway in the British Isles.

West Baldwin Reservoir

Once into the mountains there is a magic feel to the surroundings, almost an atmospheric tingle. No day in the mountains is the same as any other. The light plays on the slopes in an almost musical way; here a dark patch, there bright light and often the shadows of the clouds chasing across hillsides. All the seasons of the year have a beauty of their own in the mountains, in direct contrast to the previous or succeeding season. It is as if the peaks keep trying on new overcoats, sometimes green, at other times a multi-coloured quilted jacket. Slopes covered in heather and *ling*, the old Norse word for a heather type of plant – drifting down into bracken and gorse. The Good Lord's handiwork certainly gives great pleasure and a feeling of contentment in the Mountains of Mann.

The mountains have been guardians to the peace of the Island, serving as lookout posts in times of threat. Indeed careful perusal of the OS map will show that there is more than one mountain or hill by the name of *Cronk ny Arrey Laa*, understood to be the Hill of the Day Watch or sometimes known to the fishermen as the Hill of the Day Rise.

Valleys

There are no great valleys on the Isle of Man, the size of the Island prevents it, but the two areas of mountains are divided by the central valley running in a South East/North West direction between Douglas and Peel. Approaching the Island by sea from England the first detail seen on the landfall is the Fall of Greeba, a purple, tree clad slope that always tells Manx homecomers they are back! Greeba lies about half-way along the valley and is a splendid landmark.

Running northward to the East of the mountain are the twin valleys of East and West Baldwin.

Many rivers and streams run into these valleys which empty their waters into the Injebreck Reservoir or on to the sea. It is likely that the Baldwins were awarded valley status because of their width.

Glens

The glens of the Island with their narrow profiles far outnumber the valleys. They vary in physical dimensions by length, breadth, steepness, isolation, accessibility but not in beauty. Everyone of them has a grace of its very own. Give yourself time to reconnoitre and a favourite glen will present itself.

Many of the glens were only opened up to wheeled traffic because of the mining industry. One has to remember that the wheel only put in an appearance on the Island just over a couple of centuries ago. Pack horses and heavy wooden sledges were the main means of transporting goods about the countryside.

The rushing waters of the steep glens were put to good use; for milling and here and there you would often find washing floors for the extraction of minerals. They were also directed to drive

Glen Helen

turbines for power in the manufacture of paper. The purity of the water favoured a number of attempts at setting up a cotton industry. There were many other manufacturing uses for the glens and every one will produce ancient buildings of one sort or another, sited to improve the economic well being of the Island. It is virtually impossible on a short visit to get anything but a flavour of the history of our glens.

In more modern times the glens have become centres for leisure and a thriving government operated forestry industry. Many of the glens (seventeen) are owned by the Manx Government and in keeping with ancient rights you have free access to them. The Isle of Man Department of Agriculture, Fisheries and Forestry is responsible for the good husbandry of the public glens and they do a splendid job. A friendly word of advice if you decide on a bit of glen walking, please wear good shoes or trainers, the walking can be rough – the policy is to keep them as natural as possible. There is an excellent leaflet on glens available from the TIC's.

Our glens are divided into two types, the coastal glens and the mountain glens. Because the farmers until comparatively recent times used

Looking towards Snaefell

seaweed (locally called wrack) to fertilise their fields, access to beaches was essential and so you will find minor roads leading down to the sea. There are a number of very steep, thickly wooded, ravine-like glens with no roads. These glens are found in the main on the East coast and mostly between Douglas and Ramsey. They usually have convenient car parks. The West coast glens are generally of a more gentle nature often leading down to sandy beaches. The mountain glens are very spectacular with tumbling streams and deep, dark, rocky pools. Care must always be taken when walking the mountain glens, the footpaths can often be very slippery, particularly after a period of rain. The more lush the vegetation the more likely you are to find huge rhododendron bushes giving marvellous splashes of colour to the most out of the way places.

Parks

P arks almost seem to be a speciality of the Island. Many years ago the Founding Fathers of tourism took it upon themselves to build a great number of parks in the towns and villages. Wherever you go on the Island you will find these peaceful oases of colour. Usually the parks are operated by the local authorities but there are a number that are looked after directly by the Department of Agriculture, Fisheries and Forestry.

There are a number of private parks and gardens on the Island. Normally such places are only opened to the public for fund raising events or special occasions. One exception however is the dramatic Ballalheannagh Gardens in Glen Roy which are open all year.

St John's

Government parks such as the extensive Arboretum at St John's offer lovely well situated picnic areas. The park is full of trees and bushes, gifted to the Manx Nation by world governments in celebration of our Tynwald Millennium. Watch out for the friendly ducks however at the

Arboretum, they are probably the best fed creatures on the Island and not at all adverse at reminding you of their presence. If you are in the vicinity of St John's a good suggestion is to visit the Department's nursery gardens. You are free to wander round the gardens and you will see why we are so proud of them ... and of the good folk who work in all weathers throughout the year to give us endless hours of pleasure in the glens and parks.

Douglas

Douglas has numerous parks and gardens and has always been fortuitous in having town councillors and a well led team of excellent gardeners who appreciate the pleasure the gardens give to the citizens of the Borough and visitors to the town alike. Pride of place has to be given to the "Sunken Gardens" on Douglas Promenade. Each year the gardens are virtually redesigned and special themes are used to celebrate anniversaries etc.. Where else would you find a flower calendar which changes date every day? A walk around the town will allow you to discover places like Hutchinson Square, Woodburn Square, Hilary Park, all havens of tranquillity in the busy life of the town. Noble's Park along with the Villa Marina and its gardens was donated to the town by Henry Bloom Noble, and are renowned for their sporting facilities, offering bowls, tennis and many other leisure uses. See if you can spot the old lighthouse in the grounds of the Villa! At night, from July to October, the children love to walk down through Summer Hill Glen and delight in the fairy lights and illuminated animal displays. Douglas celebrates its centenary as a Borough in 1996 and one of the ways it is recognising this landmark is with a yellow florabunda rose. Named as "Douglas Centenary" it will be available by mail order and you will be able to see a bed of them in the Villa Marina Gardens.

Onchan

To the North end of Douglas Bay is Onchan Park. Endless fun for all the family and within walking distance of most of Douglas, hotels or why

QUALITY THAT STANDS·THE TEST OF TIME

FARM SOURCED, FARM ASSURED
TRADITIONAL MEAT
FROM
THE ISLE OF MAN

not hop on a horse tram for a relaxing ride along the Promenade. Walk up through the gardens at Port Jack, turn left at the top and Onchan Park is one minute away.

Laxey

Laxey has fine natural gardens and the children can have a wonderful time there. The site of the old mine washing floors has been turned into gardens to blend in with the surrounding landscape and offers good shelter on blustery days. The village is also close to the famous Ballalheannagh Gardens at Glen Roy. Tucked away in one of the most beautiful glens in the Island these gardens are off the beaten track but easily accessible by car, taxi or mini-bus. To find the gardens follow the B12 from Creg-ny-Baa towards Laxey and turn left just before Social Cottage. If you approach from Laxey take the Glen Roy Road which goes up the hill from the petrol station in the centre of the village. Built into steep hillsides, cleverly using every inch of the terrain with waterfalls and cascades offering scenic backdrops, the four miles of gravel paths

give access to displays of Ericaceae, Rhododendron, Eucryphia, Pieris, Betula, Alnus and Sorbus, which form the backbone of a collection numbering in excess of 10,000 different plants. Open daily from 10am. to 1pm. and again from 2pm. to 5pm. the only time the Gardens close is for ten days over the Christmas period. There is a modest admissioin charge, call 861875 for further information. This is definitely worth a visit

Ramsey

Further North in Royal Ramsey, the very fine Mooragh Park awaits you. Mingled in with the flowers and bushes, its twelve acre shallow lake offers boating facilities for young and old. There are rowing boats, canoes, pedalos and sailing dinghies for hire or you can learn to sail, canoe or windsurf with one of the experienced instructors. All these facilities are provided by Mansail at the Boathouse. They also run the bowling green, crazy golf and the putting green. Not feeling energetic! Light refreshments and ices are available for those who just want to sit and watch. The Town

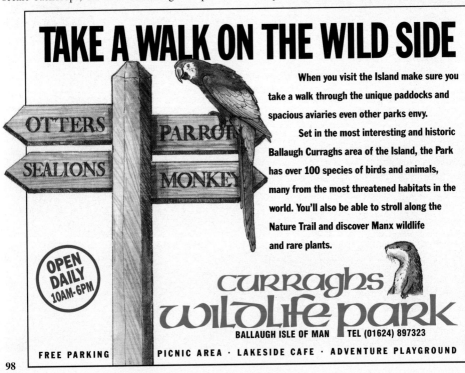

Curraghs Wildlife Park

Commissioners in conjunction with the local Rotarians have developed wasteland along the banks of the Sulby River as a natural park. Known as *Poyll Dooey*, it translates as Pool of the Black Ford and a walk through the area brings you to a ford which was the main crossing point between North and South Ramsey long before the town's bridges were built.

Curraghs

A park with a difference is the Currraghs Wildlife Park near Ballaugh, on the A3. Set in natural surroundings the theme of the park allows visitors to wander through the enclosures, observing the animals and birds at close quarters. Some animals are kept separate from their human visitors such as recent new arrivals, a pair of Indian Fishing Cats and the Lynx. There is a walk-through Aviary and an Ark which offers environmental input. The refurbished cafe has a magnificent setting on the edge of a small lake with *Mount Karrin*, St Ciaran's Mount, keeping watch above the Curraghs. Guardians of the lake are undoubtedly the Spider monkeys, just watch them control the waterfront. Besides looking for the new animals and birds, ask for a copy of the Park's new Guide Book, it's full of fascinating information. Children love the Wildlife Park with its nature trails and there are play areas designed to let them work off their surplus energy. During the summer the miniature railway "The Orchid Line" provides further diversion.

It has been mentioned elsewhere that something was stirring at the bottom of the ocean in relation to the birth of the Isle of Man. In 1885 something was also stirring in the mind of a man whose name was to become synonymous with marine biology, the Island, and particularly with Port Erin. A Professor of Natural History at the age of 23, William Herdman suggested that a committee be formed to investigate the marine biology of Liverpool Bay and its surrounding waters.

Early on in the life of this gathering of eminent scientists, work was carried out using as a base an old abandoned semaphore station on Puffin Island, a small rocky islet just off the eastern tip of Anglesey. Just five short years later their work had expanded and in 1892 a humble laboratory supported by an aquarium was opened on the South side of Port Erin Bay. From such a simple beginning a world renowned centre of excellence in the field of marine biology has been established. Operating now under the auspices of Liverpool University's Department of Oceanography, many fine scientists have been spawned here, following in the footsteps of this early leader of marine science. Knighted for his work, Sir William's name is perpetuated in Port Erin by the village library.

Above the waves

Exploration of the seas obviously needs a good sea boat and the Marine Biology Station has had the distinction of operating over the years a number of fine research vessels including the steam yacht *"Ladybird"* 1908, the *"William Herdman"*, 1948-66, the *"Cuma"*, 1966-91, and the present day vessel *"Rogan"*. Spending much of their time at sea and occasionally in waters far from the Island the crew and scientists push outwards the boundaries of knowledge of the sea and the environment. The *"Rogan"* can sometimes be seen alongside the outer breakwater at Port St Mary.

Beneath the waves

No soft options for the students of Port Erin. Every student is expected to fulfil his or her quota of research work and each year the Station, which was the first institute in Britain to offer a degree in Marine Biology, welcomes some 200 students to study the rich waters of the Isle of Man. There is also a resident population of researchers all eagerly working towards their Ph.D.s.

In the past marine biologists could only sample the make up of the undersea world by pulling dredges along or near the sea bed, a far from efficient method of studying the mysteries of the deep. Modern technological advances such as free-diving allow biologists to study beneath the waves in a whole range of areas. Pioneering work over many years by Port Erin scientists and diving staff now allows the student to study the Subtidal Margins at depths of 0-2 metres, the Kelp Forest at anything from 2 metres-15/20 metres and the Rock beyond the Forest lying at depths of 15-30 metres. Deeper still, these expert divers explore the Gravel Beds and the Mud Desert at depths of up to 50 metres.

Fishing

Traditionally the Irish Sea has been good to the Isle of Man but perhaps the writing was on the wall or at least on the surface when William Herdman was just 10 years old, for it was then that the Westminster Parliament, in the mistaken belief that the harvest from the sea was inexhaustible, repealed all laws appertaining to the control of fishing.

With the arrival of a motorised fishing fleet in the late nineteenth century, catches increased and stocks began to dwindle at an alarming rate. Remedial action was taken but this only served to slow the decline rather than halting it. In more recent times even more modern methods of fishing have driven stocks in some instances almost to the point of extinction, highlighting the importance of the work of Port Erin's Marine Biology Station in the fields of stock preservation and cultivation.

Plankton

The source of food for many creatures in the open sea is a tiny plant and animal organism generally known as Plankton. This is actually divided up as Phytoplankton (plant form) and Zoo Plankton (animal form). Drifting along in great numbers this microscopic form of nutrition feeds creatures great and small. Life in the sea is not a lot different than on the land and plankton is no exception to the rule. As the spring days grow longer the sunlight causes the Phytoplankton to bloom. With each cell multiplying and dividing until even a single litre of water contains millions of cells, the nutrients of the sea are drained, providing a productive source in the marine food chain.

Calf Sound

The Basking Shark

Plankton as the primary source of nourishment for almost all marine creatures is consumed by scampi, scallops, mussels and other crustaceans, sponges, fish larvae and small drifting animals ... but by far the greatest single consumer of plankton is the Basking shark.

Because energy is lost at each stage of the marine food chain there is very little left to support the growth of really large organisms. Enter the Basking shark, the businessman of the undersea world! No commission agents or middle men for this noble creature of the depths, just a gentle swim through a rich source of nutrition. A 35 foot long Basking shark weighing as much as a bus or

two elephants, filters in one hour the equivalent amount of water required to fill a 50 metre swimming pool.

One of the unsolved mysteries of the sea is why do these monsters of the deep choose to come to the waters of Mann each summer to feed? Come they do though ... and they appear regularly, cruising up and down our western coast feeding on the rich supplies of plankton. In the autumn they vanish just as quickly as they arrive. Many years ago a Manx scientist, Ken Watterson acting at first totally on his own and without support decided to find the answers to some of the questions puzzling the scientific world. Still researching and still learning Ken has become a leading World Authority on the Basking shark – the second largest fish known to mankind. Much valuable publicity has been generated for the Island and the original Basking Shark Project has now been enlarged and formalised as the Isle of Man Basking Shark Charitable Trust. Ken is now supported by a keen and energetic team, allowing the work to continue at a greater pace. Look out for the distinctive shark boat when you are in Peel.

Day Tours by Car

One of the amusing facts about the Isle of Man concerns the new residents and their insistence on driving for hours around the Island when they first arrive. Within a couple of weeks this energetic approach disappears and journeys around the Island are made at a much more leisurely pace.

For the visitor who likes to explore by car and has arrived on the Island independently, hiring a car gives the opportunity to get off the beaten track, and one of the best known firms in the business is Mylchreests. Hiring a car from Mylchreests is easy and gives you quality of service and the freedom to come and go as you please. The friendly folk in the hire department are pleased to assist in any way they can. Should you require a baby/child seat this can be supplied ... and there is no charge, but please try and give them a little bit of advance notice and an idea of the children's ages. Arrangements can be made to meet you at the Sea Terminal or to deliver a car to your hotel or accommodation, and their Airport Office is open for all confirmed arrivals. If you need advice on getting around the Island or have arrived without pre-booking any accommodation, don't worry ask the Mylchreests, staff they will be glad to help.

More and more of our visitors are taking advantage of car rental and the connections that this prominent company have on a world-wide basis means that they can easily match up your specifications. Simply phone or fax your requirements to Mylchreests and this will take care of even the most complicated arrangements.

There is a good range of cars in the Mylchreests, fleet to suit most tastes and pockets, and there are a number of choices relating to hire periods. If you don't need a car for the whole of your stay then ask about the special Weekenders or Week Specials. The team will gladly tailor a package to suit you, and by the way, ask them about the Isle of Man's Magnetic Hill, it's fun with a car! There is no-one who knows the roads of Mann better than them. The service also includes a free Isle of Man map and a useful road map of Douglas.

The Island has had to succumb to very few of the pressures of modern life. Driving a car is still pleasurable but as with many places the yellow paint brigade have been about. Double and single yellow lines have precisely the same meaning as in the UK and elsewhere. Do not be mislead into thinking that they are merely a measurement of distance from the kerb! Help is at hand though as every Mylchreests' car comes supplied with a parking disc and it is really only in the more built up areas that you need the discs.

Mylchreests have sponsored half a dozen drives in this guide. The routes cover most regions in the Isle of Man and are designed to be enjoyed at a leisurely pace, giving ample opportunity to visit points of interest along the way. The accompanying maps should be sufficient for the purpose, but more detailed information can of course be found on the Ordnance Survey Map of the Isle of Man. Please bear in mind that although the country areas are well served by petrol stations, there are districts where they are spaced a good distance apart.

Mylchreests are definitely one of the better ways to get to know the Island.

CAR RENTAL

MYLCHREESTS

SUPER SUMMER DRIVES

GROUP	WEEKEND PER DAY		WEEKLY	
	CAR	£	CAR	£
X	ROVER 100 3 Door	17.25	ROVER 100 3 Door	99.00
A	ROVER 100 5 Door	18.75	ROVER 100 5 Door	111.00
B	ROVER 200 5 Door	20.00	ROVER 200 5 Door	125.00
C	ROVER 400 5 Door	21.25	ROVER 400 5 Door	145.00
E	MONTEGO ESTATE	23.75	MONTEGO ESTATE	185.00

- Weekend rentals any time Friday to anytime Monday minimum 3 days within office hours
- Child/Baby seats available
- Rover Automatic and Minibus available Tel for quote
- All rates include full insurance (NO EXCESS) and V.A.T. as at 01.08.95
- Cars available from our Sea Terminal or Airport offices

All drivers must be over 23 and under 75 and have held a full drivers licence for over 1 year. Please advise on any endorsements.

I wish to book the following vehicle (Please Tick)

❑ **Rover 100** 3Dr ❑ **Rover 100** 5DR ❑ **Rover 200** ❑ **Rover 400**
❑ **Montego Estate** ❑ I am interested in an 8 seater Minibus

Name... Depart from.........................Air/SeaPort
Address...................................... Flight No..
.............................Post Code................... Arrival IOM date.................Time............
Tel... Depart IOM date.................Time............

Please note: Full confirmation and conditions for this booking will be sent to you.
If you wish to discuss your booking and availability details telephone 01624 828533
All services and special offers subject to availability

Cars available from our offices at the Sea Terminal or Airport

All booking enquiries to:-
Ronaldsway Airport Ballasalla Isle of Man IM9 2AS

☎ **01624 823533**

Tour 1

Douglas: Signpost Corner: The Bungalow: Ramsey: Maughold: Port Mooar: Port Cornaa: Dhoon: Laxey **Miles 35**

As the vast majority of the Island's visitors stay on or near Douglas seafront, we will start Tour 1 at the foot of Broadway, which is adjacent to the Villa Marina or just about where the Harris Promenade merges with Central Promenade.

The Villa Marina has been in the forefront of the Manx tourism scene for many decades, putting on from time to time shows, stars of music and dancing, ballroom dancing and popular family entertainment. It is built on land donated by a much loved citizen of the town, Henry Bloom Noble who, as a young man acting on his own initiative, bought a cargo of timber for his employer who was away on business. Alas for the employer he repudiated the young Noble's deal and thus set him on his way as a rival to fame and fortune with the proceeds of the sale of what had now become his goods. It's a good place to start our drive. The gardens at the Villa are attractive and a popular place for the visitor to watch the world pass by is from the roof of the Villa Marina Colonnade, entrance being gained from the gardens. After serving the Island well for many decades the Villa will soon be undergoing a major face lift in preparation for its life in the next century.

Climbing up Broadway we start to leave the tourist part of town behind and as Broadway becomes Ballaquayle Road we find ourselves at the Bray Hill traffic lights – turn right and head past the TT Grandstand (on your right). Some three quarters of a mile along Glencrutchery Road you arrive at Governor's Bridge. Be careful here that you don't turn too quickly, and take care at the double roundabout before following the road marked Ramsey, turning up by the white painted stone wall. For the next few hundred yards on the right you are passing the home of the Island's Governor. Head on up the A18 to Signpost Corner,

it's open country after this. Leaving Cronk-ny-Mona behind there is a distinct change of scenery starting to take place as the road winds upwards to the famous TT viewing spot of Creg-ny-Baa. Over to your left as Kate's Cottage comes into sight are some very good views of Douglas and the panorama of the southern half of the Isle of Man lies before you. Please be very careful where you stop to view, especially on the TT Course as it is a very fast road. Passing through Keppel Gate you are now in the mountains and into some of the finest scenery in the British Isles.

Still on the A18 we start our descent to Ramsey at Brandywell, just past the junction with the B10. Directly in front of you stands proud Snaefell and if time permits it is well worth stopping here and catching an electric tram to the summit. It is a fact that on a clear day seven Kingdoms can be seen from the top of the mountain. Not sure if this isn't a Manx fairy tale? Well, there before you lie the Kingdoms of England, Wales, Scotland, Ireland, Mann, the Kingdom of the Sea ... and the Kingdom of Heaven.

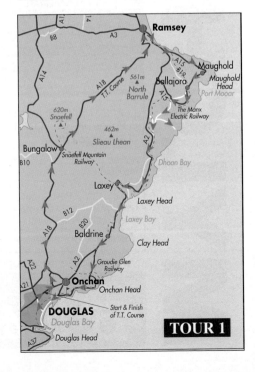

Ramsey

In 1995 the Snaefell Mountain railway celebrated its centenary and what's more with the original rolling stock still in use. Past Snaefell the magnificent mountain scenery continues with the views on your right of Laxey and its valley gradually giving way to the stunning sight of Ramsey and the northern plain spreading out before you. Ramsey is a place well worth exploring and as ever Mylchreests' cars are supplied with parking discs just in case you don't find a disc free park. If you are driving your own vehicle, discs are available on the ferries, from TIC's or many public offices and police stations.

Maughold is the next stop on our itinerary and we find our way there by driving along Ramsey Promenade and past the Queen's Pier, watching for the signs directing traffic to Laxey A2. We are not on the A2 for long before we bear left onto the A15. A good tip on these roads is to watch out for the un-manned tram crossings as you will be criss-crossing them for the next few miles. About half a mile past Maughold there is a small road which takes you down onto the beach at Port Mooar. Don't expect to find any ships here but you will find peace and tranquillity. It's an ideal place to stretch your legs and have a picnic. Back up from the beach we turn left onto the A15 and travel to Cornaa.

If you like ancient monuments there is a well preserved burial ground just past the Ballajora crossroads – there is an old chapel on the corner, keep that to the left and travel up hill on the minor road – which in more recent times became the last resting place for those Quakers who remained on the Island, the majority of their fellow believers escaping persecution by seeking a new life in America. Careful navigation is required approaching Cornaa as the roads are very narrow. Turn off the A15 at Cornaa tram halt and turn down the minor road to the left. Pass the Ballaglass Glen car park on your right and drive on until you reach a small ford where you turn right for Port Cornaa. This is a very tight corner and you may feel happier by driving up the road a little way to turn. The drive down to the beach is well worth the effort but be careful where you park, it is a popular spot with locals and sometimes the stony upper beach can cause problems if you pick the wrong place.

When coming back up this lovely wooded valley continue past the ford – on your right – and climb back up onto the A2 watching out for the signs to the Dhoon and Laxey. If you are feeling energetic park opposite the Dhoon station and enjoy a walk down to the shore but remember to leave extra time for the return journey ... it can kid

Laxey harbour

105

you. The A2 soon takes the happy traveller to Laxey and there are spectacular views all along the coast. Laxey has so much to offer that anything less than a prolonged visit, borders on neglect. Enjoy the village because there is something new to see on each visit. There is a choice on how you leave. If you are in Old Laxey then the steep road up from the harbour soon comes out on the A2 at Fairy Cottage, or if you have been exploring in the vicinity of the mines then rejoin by the Electric Railway station. On through the picturesque villages of Lonan, Garwick and Baldrine and over the tram crossing just out of Baldrine, taking a left turn and over a second crossing in the vicinity of the Halfway House to Laxey (Liverpool Arms) – the road A11 is signposted to Groudle and Douglas. Groudle is another good place to while away a happy hour or two with its beautiful natural glen and the revitalised miniature Groudle Railway. Almost home but not finished with the scenery. Stop a while and drink in the sight of beautiful Douglas Bay. Day or night, you will enjoy the view.

St John's

Tour 2

Douglas: East Baldwin: Injebreck: Druidale: Ballaugh: Kirk Michael: Peel: St. John's **Miles 38**

This journey takes as its starting point the bottom of Broadway and proceeds in just the same manner as that described in Drive 1, until the traffic lights at Parkfield Corner (St. Ninian's Church) are reached. Get into the filter left lane and enjoy the run down Bray Hill to the bottom of the dip where you take a right turn – it's easy to spot – look out for Bradley's grocery shop. Allow yourself a brief thought for the racing motor cyclists as they speed down that hill at over 150 mph!

The road now winds along through an area known as *Port-e-Chee*, which translated from the Gaelic means Haven of Peace, and it needs little imagination to realise that this place may well have been, in pre-glacial times, the site of one of the

earliest harbours in the Isle of Man. Cronkbourne Village is the next destination and this is soon reached. Turn right and go up the steep Johnny Watterson's Lane A21 turning left at the halt sign, then drive along Ballanard Road A22 towards Abbeylands for just over a mile. At the crossroads turn left and heading over Sir George's Bridge make a right turn onto the B21, the East Baldwin Road.

It is very hard to imagine that between 1900-05 a narrow three foot gauge railway wound its way around these small valleys busily carrying workers and building materials for the Injebreck Reservoir. Keep on the B21 and move in a northerly direction until you reach the old and disused East Baldwin Chapel. Park here awhile and if you are not blessed with sharp eyes use binoculars to see if you can spot "The White Man of East Baldwin". The "White Man" is a figure built into a mountain wall on the hillside as a memorial to a Deemster, who perished with his horse in a snowstorm, whilst on an errand of mercy. The walk up to the cairn from the bottom of the valley is strenuous, and mind you don't get your feet wet when crossing the Baldwin River. Any physical discomfort experienced on the way up is soon overcome and the views are more than adequate compensation for the effort.

Retrace your track back to Algare Hill – it's the small connecting road between the two valleys – and a right turn at the top brings you along to St Luke's Church which is on the site of an ancient Tynwald. Drop down to the valley floor and join the B22 by heading once more in a northerly direction. Lots of nice picnic spots around here but do be careful where you park, the roads are narrow. If you like to fish then the appropriate licences are available from the Douglas TIC, Department of Agriculture, Fisheries and Forestry or some local Post Offices ... and Injebreck is as good a place as anywhere to indulge. From the reservoir the road climbs up between the peaks of Colden and Carraghan eventually bringing you out onto the Brandywell Road B10. Just before the junction there is a small slip road which you should turn into and, by turning right and then almost straight

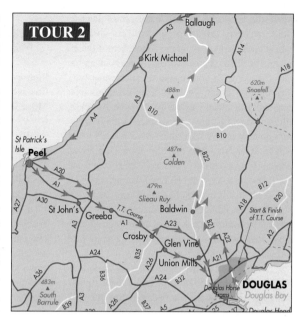

away left, you are now on the Druidale Road. This is a single track road for its entire length. If you decide to stop and admire the views, park the car to one side and please watch out for sheep and cattle they have the run of the range up here on the moors. A short drive down Ballaugh Glen brings the traveller to the village.

Turning left at the famous Ballaugh Bridge puts you onto the A3. The car driver has the advantage over the TT riders because at least the wheels stay firmly on the ground – the leather clad heroes are airborne for quite a distance here. Now we are heading South West towards Kirk Michael, home of Runic Crosses and the last resting place of no less than five bishops. Take the right fork here as the A3 becomes the A4 and we head down towards the sunset city of Peel. This is a good road but if you are not in a hurry then enjoy a flask of tea or coffee at Glen Wyllin, Glen Mooar or the Devil's Elbow. By now the visitor to our fair shores will have gathered that much of the beauty of the Island requires a Mylchreests' car or your own vehicle to get the best out of a visit.

Peel is a place to visit with time to spend on exploring. This is the only "city" on the Island – two cathedrals make sure of that ranking – a title of

Manx Post Box

which the good citizens are justly proud. Peel is close to every Manx person's heart so give yourselves time to soak up the atmosphere. Lots of interesting shops, narrow streets, a harbour and a very fine castle. If you are out on an evening run, stay for the sunset, you won't be disappointed. Leaving Peel behind we take the A1 to St. John's, a village of great political importance in the lives of our modern nation. An alternative route to the village is via the A20 and the connecting road through Tynwald Mills ... it is well signposted from Peel. Alongside Tynwald Hill and the memories of past deeds that it evokes, lies the Royal Chapel of St. John. The village is little changed in the best part of a century, representing as it does all the things that the Manx most cherish ... freedom, law and order, and tradition.

The last part of the drive takes us along the central valley. Hard to imagine that a mere 10,000 years ago this was the sea bed, dividing the two main parts of the Isle of Man from each other. Moving along the A1 towards Ballacraine we come up against that rarity in the Island, a set of traffic lights. Carry straight on towards Douglas but just after Greeba Castle look to your left and there is the ancient roofless church of St. Trinian standing in splendid isolation in its own meadow. There is a choice of routes to the capital from here on.

The main road follows the A1 to the Sea Terminal via Glen Vine, Union Mills, Braddan Bridge, and the Quarter Bridge. Alternatively if time permits why not take the A23, the Nab Road, by turning left at Crosby and heading towards Douglas via Eyreton, the Nab, the Strang and Braddan – the A23 rejoins the A1 at the Jubilee Oak Braddan Bridge. If it's dark when arriving back in the metropolis, enjoy the promenade lights.

Tour 3

Ramsey: Point of Ayre: Jurby: The Cronk: The Curraghs: Sulby: Tholt-e-Will: The Bungalow
Miles 38

For those visitors staying in Ramsey there are many pleasant drives to enjoy in the close vicinity of this small market town. The drive described in the following few paragraphs will just emphasise the kaleidoscope of choice that faces the visitor to Ellan Vannin. A car makes that choice all the more exciting and the writer feels and hopes that in the few miles described in Drive 3 the tourist will feel something of the changeability of the Island that can only best be described as the "Magic of Mann".

As you wander around the great northern plain the scenery changes frequently, from the fine sands of the Lhen, gravel beaches of the Point of Ayre, up to the wooded slopes of Sky Hill, Glen Auldyn, *Carrick*, Rock and *Mount Karrin*, St. Ciaran's

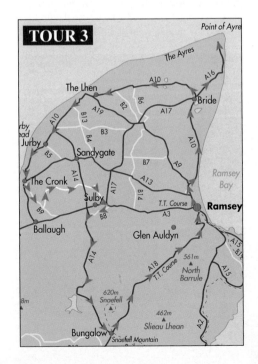

Mount. Coupled with the winding lanes of the Curraghs it is one of the best places to tour. The drive starts on Ramsey Promenade but before setting off be sure to take in the lovely sight of the bay and the slopes of *Liargee Frissel*, Frissel's slope – it's the hill with the tower set on the summit.

Driving along the Mooragh Promenade gives you a feeling of a bygone age when there was time aplenty. You may even be rewarded with a glimpse of St. Bee's Head in Cumberland, the nearest point any of the adjacent islands come to the Isle of Man. At the end of the Promenade bear left up the hill and join the A10 by turning right. Follow this road to the lovely village of Bride. The church acts as a good landmark for miles around, so if you feel the need for a little guidance, keep your eyes on the spire, it is easy to lose one's bearings in the far North. At Bride take the A16 marked for the Point of Ayre. Again it is an easy place to find because the lighthouse stands as a sentinel for sailors and landlubbers alike. This landmark was built in the early years of last century by the great-grandfather of Robert Louis Stevenson well known of course to lovers of adventure stories. Definitely not the place to go swimming, the waters surrounding the Point are some of the most treacherous in the world.

On now to the Lhen, so reverse the route back as far as Bride and turn right and West at the church. Lovely country here with good farming land rolling down to the coast. Watch out for the sign to the Ayres Visitor Centre, well worth a visit; open from mid-May to mid-September between the hours of 2-5pm, Wednesdays to Sundays. Stay on the A10 and the Lhen is reached after a pleasant drive of a few miles. Watch out for the sharp turn at the Lhen Bridge. If you are fond of beach picnics then the little park close to the shore is ideal – but don't lose your car keys, especially if it's a Mylchreests car – it is a long way to a garage! Just a couple of miles further on, is Jurby. This village long ago was important for the Vikings and although it has lost something of its old eminence it is nonetheless a pleasant part of our land and well worth exploring for its beaches, church and crosses. Carrying on still further on the A10 we are on the look out for *The Cronk*, The Hill, such as it

Point of Ayre Lighthouse

is. Go straight on here at the crossroads following the B9 and turn left at the second road down from The Cronk crossroads ... don't count any farm tracks or lanes. If you have got it right, it should be the yellow coloured road on the map taking you towards *Dollagh Mooar*, Black Lake and the *Curraghs*, Mire or Marsh. Caution here because the roads are extremely narrow and there are lots of ditches awaiting the careless driver. Cross the A14, approximately half way between Sandygate to the North and Sulby to the South – and you are still following the yellow road to Kella and West Sulby.

Turn left at the junction and for a brief distance you are on the TT course on the famous Sulby Straight A3. Just past Sulby Bridge is the Ginger Hall public house and you should turn right here onto the B8 which will fetch you onto the *Sulby Claddaghs*, the River Meadowland. The Claddaghs hold affectionate memories for generations of the Manx, happy reminders of family and Sunday School picnics, camping and more. Leaving memories and picnics behind, we move through the Claddaghs to the A14 or the Sulby Glen Road and begin the ascent of the glen towards Tholt-e-Will. This extremely scenic route brings you up

Looking South from Jurby Head

past the Sulby Reservoir built in the early eighties with an eye to securing our water supplies well into the next century. Watch out for sheep on this road, they are not always party to the good custom and practice of the Highway Code. The upper reaches of the road roll across the shoulder of Snaefell and the scenery is typical of high moorland interspersed with plantation.

The end of the A14 joins the A18 TT course at the Bungalow. There is an Electric Railway station here and during the season the Snaefell Mountain Railway operates regular services between Snaefell summit and Laxey far below at the bottom of the valley. Turn left and travel the "wrong way" around the TT course, it is still a fast stretch of road and in high winds or misty conditions it is a place to be avoided. The bonus of the road is to be found in clear weather, summer or winter, with fine views of the Ayres, Scotland, England and Ireland. Please take care on the final descent into Ramsey, there are some sharp corners. Once into Royal Ramsey the final destination is yours, it is an easy town to find your way about and the A18 takes the driver right into Parliament Square. Turn right just

through the Square and you are into Derby Road and West Quay. Cross the Swing Bridge and the Mooragh Promenade awaits.

Tour 4

Peel: St. John's: Cronk-y-Voddy: West Baldwin: Ballasalla: Castletown: Foxdale **Miles 40**

Peel is a must for all visitors and if you are not actually staying there then an early visit should be a high priority. Mylchreests Drive 4 will take you from Peel through the Island's lovely hinterland, taking in moorland, valleys and glens. We take as our starting point the north end of Peel Promenade in the vicinity of the Empire Garage and proceed up Stanley Road turning right then almost immediately left into Church Street. At the halt sign – you will observe Peel Police Station across the road – take a left and head into Derby Road and the A20 signposted for St. John's. You will know that you have the right road when you pass the

Poortown quarry and after about a mile and a half turn right down the small road marked Tynwald Craft Centre. This is a development that the Isle of Man can consider justifiably to be one of the jewels in the crown and it is well worth allowing plenty of time for a stop here.

Leave the Tynwald Craft Centre complex by the opposite end and bear left onto the TT course, the A3. Warning! The exit onto the main road is narrow and sometimes approaching cars from your right hand side may be travelling at speed. Now you are heading up the beautiful wooded Glen Helen road and if you still feel like stretching your legs, stop awhile and stroll up the glen. From opposite the glen car park the road climbs steeply for a short distance passing the famous TT landmark Sarah's Cottage, on up *Creg Willeys Hill*, Willy Syl's or Sylvester's Crag and on to *Cronk-y-Voddy*, which translated from the Manx means the Hill of the Dog. Here at the crossroads we turn right and leave civilisation behind for a little while as we head up hill and down dale to Little London. No big city traffic problems here, but do watch out for approaching traffic as it is only a minor road.

Little London long ago was famous for fishing but nowadays its peace and tranquillity is only disturbed by the occasional passing car, or the rambler who braves the strenuous hill walks and almost stumbles on it by chance. Before the last war, the Old Smithy was the home of the famous flyer Captain Pixton who was the first British winner of the prestigious Schneider Trophy and the holder of many flying records. The road out of Little London skirts the South West slopes of *Sartfell*, which is old Norse for Black Mountain or Dark Slope. In Manx it is known as *Slieau Dhoo* and joins the B10 about half a mile above *Bayr Garrow*, Rough Road.

Just before the minor road joins the main road is Sartfield Farmhouse Restaurant (See Advert on Page76). If you are from an older generation you will remember the old style farmhouse food, if you are from a younger age group then you will have nothing to lose by breaking the journey at this delightful place and eating your fill. Exciting days ahead for Sartfield as they plan the expansion of their business; more room in the restaurant, six en-

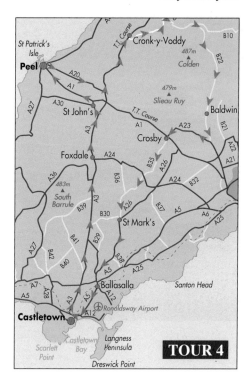

TOUR 4

suite bedrooms plus a residents lounge and dining room ... all designed to keep them up there with the leaders. Don't miss the views, at anytime of day or night the scenery is fabulous and from this unique vantage point on a fine evening the flashing lighthouses of Northern Ireland and the Mull of Galloway in Scotland can clearly be seen.

Turn up the hill and on the way look back at the view; on clear days there are fine panoramic images of the Mountains of Mourne and the Mull of Galloway. You are now heading along the Brandywell Road with Colden Mountain ahead and to the right. There are a lot of cattle grids in the mountains so be sure to take care crossing them and if you have to use the gates, please don't forget to close them after use. Keep a look out for the B22 turning; it should be easy to spot because it is just before Brandywell Cottage, and that is the only building on the left since you started on the B10. Turn off to the right and head along the Injebreck Road, and if you want a good idea of what the centre of the Island looks like, pull in just before

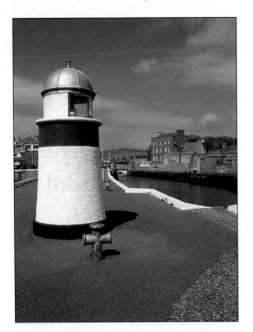

Castletown

the crest of the hill and you will see a countryside little changed since the end of the Ice Age.

Heading down into the West Baldwin valley is a pleasant experience evoking, for many, memories of driving in the Scottish Highlands. At the upper end of this green and treelined cleft, *Carraghan* stands sentinel. When first you spot this peak, realisation will dawn that the old Manx inhabitants knew what they were doing when they named the mountain – in English it means rough, craggy or rocky place. It was chosen as an ideal spot for the Injebreck Reservoir which has served Douglas and much of the Island for many decades. On down the valley, keep to the B22 all the way until Mount Rule halt sign, where a right turn puts the motorist onto the A23 bound for the central village of Crosby. Hard to imagine that the road you are following would, in an era of long ago, have been edging along the South coast of the larger of the two northern islands that made up the Isle of Man at the time of the last Ice Age.

Go straight across the Crosby crossroads and up the B35 towards St Mark's. It is likely that at one time a cross stood somewhere near the site of the present day village, because its name is derived from the Scandinavian word for Cross Village or Farm. The Mylchreests route is now taking you on one of the drivable parts of the Millennium Way. In 1979 the Manx Nation gave itself a present to commemorate 1,000 years of unbroken parliamentary rule and if you feel that you have not yet really stretched your legs since arriving on our shores ... then try walking the full distance, it's only twenty eight miles!

St Mark's is a quiet little backwater and lies peacefully on a rise, giving it the status of a landmark for ramblers, cyclists and motorists alike, visible for a good distance around the parish of Malew. Once a year it comes to life with the holding of the ancient St Mark's Fair. A couple of miles or so further on you come to the busy village of Ballasalla. In more recent times there has been an upsurge in commercial activities here and the little village school does sterling work in preparing the children for senior school and life in the outside world. There is plenty to do in Ballasalla and if you are hungry by now, there are no better places to eat your fill than by visiting one or other of the pubs or restaurants in the village. If you have children in the car take a diversion just as you are coming into Ballasalla and enjoy the delights of Silverdale Glen – it is well signposted.

As you come into the centre of the village there are a couple of roundabouts to circumnavigate, take care as there can be exciting moments experienced on them. Driving directions require you to go straight on at each roundabout looking for the Airport and Castletown signs, the A5. Pass the Airport on your left and drive into Castletown. The old Capital is described in detail elsewhere and it is well worth planning a prolonged visit. This is a disc parking area so don't forget to place it in a clear position on the dashboard.

The journey back to Peel is fairly straight forward. Retrace the route back along the harbour in Castletown to Victoria Road and the first roundabout, where you should turn left into Alexander Road, crossing over the Alexander Bridge. Carry on for a quarter of a mile and turn right into Malew Road and the A3. Stay on the A3, climbing up the Ballamodha Straight before dropping down through the old mining villages of Upper and Lower Foxdale. Approaching St John's the road divides at a small hamlet called The Hope – don't worry it is not shown on many maps – take the left branch and follow the A30 past the Forestry Board's nurseries, bearing right until you reach the halt sign in the middle of the village. A good guide if you are on the correct route is that Tynwald Hill is across the road. Turn left at St John's for Peel and follow the A1 and the signs all the way to Peel Promenade and the end of Drive 4.

Tour 5

Port Erin: The Slogh: Niarbyl: Glen Maye: Foxdale: Braaid: Douglas: Ballasalla: Port St. Mary: Cregneash **Miles 42**

Port Erin is a good place to base yourself for a motoring holiday, be it with your own vehicle or a Mylchreests hire car. Parking is easy and although parts of the village are disc zones, they present no real difficulties to the visitor. This drive is started on the Upper Promenade in the vicinity of one of the Port Erin Group of Hotels and will cover the southern portion of the Island. It is a journey that will take you from the steep cliffs and hills of the South West, through the gentle rolling hills of Glenfaba, Rushen and Middle Sheadings to the Capital, and on to the old Manx hill village of Cregneash.

Drive up the hill away from the hotels and look for the signposts to Bradda. The village nestles on the slopes of Bradda Head and is divided into West and East, although the exact boundary between them is now somewhat blurred. This is the A32 and it brings you along a gradually widening road to *Ballafesson*, which appears on the ancient manorial roll as MacPherson's Farm. At the junction we pick up the A7 for a short while and at the next crossroads – marked as a roundabout – we turn left on the A36, up through *Ballakillowey*, McGillowey's Farm. It should be noted that the

Manx usually exchanged the prefix Mac for the prefix Balla as far as place names were concerned. Just before the junction with the B44 is reached, there is a nice open picnic area.

If it is not too early for a rest, stop here, have a flask of coffee or tea, drink in the views over Castletown Bay, and take in the sweep of the coast right round to the villages of The Howe and Cregneash high up on the Mull Peninsula. These are the ancestral lands of the writer's wife and as such remain a firm favourite for the views and the history of the area. Driving on ever upwards on this, the Slogh Road, the driver and passengers are continually rewarded with different aspects of this particularly fine landscape around almost every corner. There are many fine walks and for the less energetic, there can hardly be any better places on the Island for picnics. It is an area that probably satisfies the argument as to whether a car is needed on a visit to Ellan Vannin. Even on a short visit, it is well worth hiring a Mylchreets car just to take in the views you can witness on this particular drive.

The Slogh Road takes you to the Round Table crossroads, shades of King Arthur here? Indeed not so very long ago, a famous American academic proved to a lot of people's satisfaction that this sixth century legendary British king and Camelot were as one with the Isle of Man. Who knows for sure, but little of the area has changed in the intervening centuries and with just a tiny bit of imagination...! Turn sharp left here onto the A27 and down to *Niarbyl*. Descending the hill into Dalby village, it is easy to see whence the name for Niarbyl is derived. Jutting out into the clear waters of the Irish Sea is a tail of rocks and that is precisely how *Niarbyl* translates into English. If you have stopped at the nearby Ballacallin Hotel for lunch, then it may be helpful to walk your meal off by enjoying a visit to Niarbyl. Take the minor road down to the shore and while away the time on the rocky beach at the foot of the cliffs.

From Dalby the A27 continues on to *Glen Maye*, loosely translated meaning Yellow Glen on account of the muddy, almost clay coloured waters of the streams running down the glen. If time permits, there are a number of easy walks here, but if it is on you want to go, then proceed to the

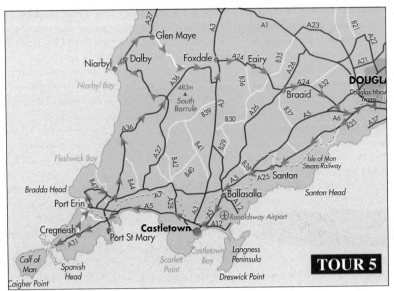

TOUR 5

over and drive to *Kewaigue*, which translates into Little Hollow. If you would like to re-visit Douglas, continue on into town, if not then just past the new Isle of Man Breweries headquarters, turn through an acute right hander and head for Santon on the A25.

Santon – in older times it was spelt Santan – derives its name from Saint Sanctan but further identification of this saintly figure and his "living" has proved difficult for the modern scholar. This road is known as the Old Castletown Road and there are a number of roads leading off it down to rocky bays and isolated coves. Try them when you have time, most are off the beaten track and are not accessible by public transport. The road takes you in the direction of Ballasalla and rejoins the A5 at a spot where the railway line passes under the main road. Stay on the A5 by turning left at the Ballasalla roundabout – the Whitestone Inn faces you directly ahead as you approach it. Drive past the Airport and skirt the edge of Castletown. Leave the town behind by using the bypass, it's still the A5, drive all the way along the edge of *Bay ny Carrickey*, The Bay of the Rock, and turn right up past the tall stone building along Beach Road, heading for the crossroads, where you go straight on using the A31. Ignore any other roads and make for Cregneash. Plenty to see here, and when you have had your fill, carry on down to The Calf Sound to enjoy the totally unspoiled scenery of the Isle of Man's equivalent of Lands End.

The final stages of the drive see us returning back up the hill from The Sound towards Cregneash again. Just before entering the village

village post office. To the side of the building there is a narrow country lane which takes you up towards *Garey*, rough or rugged river-shrubbery. Care is needed when traversing this road. Up here on the high ground, if there ever was a river, it has long since disappeared! Perhaps the road was the river, because in wet winter weather the road does seem to double as a stream. There is another name for this road, the Back of the Moon Road and as it is a lonely place, be sure you have plenty of fuel. Rushen Mines soon loom up and even the isolation of the mines have a particular beauty of their own. Back onto the A36 with a left turn and down the mountain to South Barrule Plantation and the junction with the A3. Head left towards Foxdale where you take the first right and join the A24. Skirt the edge of the Eairy Dam – watch out for the ducks crossing the road - and on to *The Braaid*, literally translated it means throat or windpipe as applied in the sense of a glen or sheltered vale. This tiny collection of houses plays host to a favourite beauty spot for locals and visitors alike. Proceed straight on at the roundabout, head up the hill about half a mile, and look down and across into the central valley. The view here is known as the Plains of Heaven ... enjoy it!

Carry on this road until you arrive at a major road junction where the A24 bisects the A5, cross from the South, turn sharp left onto the minor road leading past Mull Hill and its stone circles. Dating from Neolithic times, this unspoilt area remains much as the earliest inhabitants would have known it. Almost home, but take care, this is a single track road with passing places. Port Erin nestles quietly below as you drive down Dandy Hill and onto the Lower Promenade.

Tour 6

Onchan: Baldrine: Laxey: Glen Roy: The Bungalow: Sulby: St. Judes: Andreas: Bride: Ramsey: The Gooseneck: The Hibernian: Dhoon: **Laxey Miles 49**

Onchan started life as a small village to the North of Douglas and has in recent times seen a growth outstripping that of the modern day capital. Unsuspecting souls could almost be forgiven for thinking that it is a suburb of Douglas, but the good citizens of the village have their own local government and are intensely proud of their separate existence.

We will start our drive at Onchan Head, just above Port Jack. Follow the A11 as it runs parallel to the tram track, passing as you go Groudle Glen. There is a minor road off to the right, approximately half a mile past Groudle Station and a detour up this road will bring the motorist to Old Kirk Lonan Church, well worth a visit. Completing the detour brings you out onto the A2 just to the South of Baldrine village. Carry on towards Laxey via Fairy Cottage and Old Laxey Hill – bear to the right at the Filling Station – and the quaint harbour awaits you. *Laxey* owes its origins to the Norsemen who named it Salmon River. Give yourself time here or, at the very least, a promise to return for a longer visit. From the harbour travel up the glen besides the river and when you reach the woollen mills, go up the hill, under the railway bridge and straight on at the stop sign looking for the Creg-ny-Baa signpost. You are now on the Glen Roy Road (coloured yellow on the OS map) and about to experience one of the best glen drives on the

Island. The glen was formed by the waters cascading down from *Mullagh Ouyr, Slieau Meayll*, Dun Summit, Bare or Bald Mountain and Windy Corner respectively. Look out for the Ballalheannagh Gardens they are worth a visit. Care on this road is required as there are a number of blind corners, and the road is extremely narrow in places. Eventually you rejoin a wider road, the B12 just above Social Cottage, and by turning in a South West (right) direction, the road brings you to the well known Keppel Hotel at Creg-ny-Baa. Turn right and head the "wrong way" round the TT course, the A18, aiming for the Bungalow. Just past Brandywell is the highest point on the course at almost 1,400 feet above sea level.

The Bungalow actually bears no resemblance to a modern building of that name and the current site was home, until fairly recently, to a magnificent hotel made of wood and galvanised sheeting – very popular with TT fans. Watch out for the directions to Sulby and turn left on the A14. If your companions fancy some fresh air, pull up at the top entrance to *Tholt-e-Will Glen*. Give them half an hour or so to walk the glen and pick them up just outside the inn at the bottom of the hill. However if a picnic is the order of the day then drive into the Sulby Reservoir car park and you will not be disappointed with the views. The name of the glen translated from the Manx means Hill of the Cattlefold, and the inhabitants of the lower end of the bigger glen have traditionally been known as the Sulby Cossacks. At any time of the year, Sulby Glen has a beauty all of its own. In the spring the East side of the glen colours itself with a blue haze as the bluebells fight each other for space. At other times the heather and gorse lend their own particular splash of colour and always the light creates a special atmosphere.

A quarter of the way down the glen from the inn lies Irishman's Cottage and, high above the nearby waterworks, is the small feeder reservoir of *Block Eary*. The reservoir was built up in modern times by German POW's and although it is a strenuous walk, those who partake will be rewarded with a sense of achievement. The name has changed somewhat from the original Scandinavian spelling *Blakkarg* but the meaning is

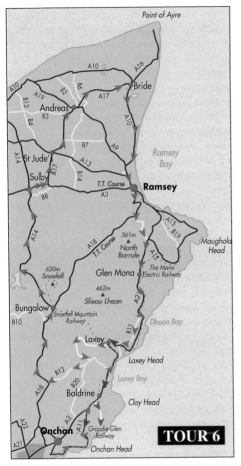

TOUR 6

marsh land.

Andreas has a fine church dedicated to Saint Andrew from whom the parish takes its name. The village is very much the centre of local agricultural activities. Leave Andreas by continuing on the same road which takes you to the Island's northernmost centre of population, Bride. The village lies in a little hollow of the Bride Hills and is one of the sunniest places on the Isle of Man according to the local meteorological office. Leaving Bride behind us, we move along the A10 in the direction of Ramsey The Bride road takes you right into Parliament Square and if you are not breaking your journey in Ramsey, a town which is highly recommended, then carry on following the route marked for the TT Course and Douglas. High above the town at the Gooseneck there is a minor road leading off behind the marshals' shelter. Careful negotiation of the turn is required to get onto what is known as the Hibernian Road. This is a delightful run across the lower slopes of *North Barrule* and whilst there seems to be no trace of the name's origination, it is most likely that it takes its form from the same meaning as *South Barrule*,

still the same, Black Sheiling, from the peaty colour of the stream.

Proceed on down the valley towards the Sulby Straight. If you feel the need for some refreshment the Peppermill Restaurant at Sulby Mill comes recommended. Carl and his hardworking staff are open seven nights a week during the summer months, and they will see you well fed for the next stage of your drive. From the Sulby Mill go straight on to the main road and turn right onto the TT Course at Sulby Methodist Church. At the end of the Straight turn off the A3 onto the St Judes Road, the A17. From the West Craig crossroads stay on the A17 to Andreas. There is a subtle change in the scenery here as the land changes from moor and glen to low lying, well drained

Plains of Heaven

Ward Mountain, a name which has close connections with the ancient system of "Watch and Ward".

As you come off this road at the Hibernian, turn right onto the A2, the Coast Road, and head for the *Corrany*. This name is a variation of *Cornaa* which means Treen, the modern version of homestead. At the *Dhoon*, Fort Quarterland, which probably took its name from the nearby earthworks of *Kionehenin*, The Head of the Precipice, you can always stop and let your passengers return by tram to Onchan. So your Mylchreests car and the dedicated drives are hopefully going to prove useful in more ways than one. Leave the Dhoon car park area by the B11, the *Ballaragh Road*. This is an interesting name and although its derivation is doubtful, there is reason to believe that perhaps its original meaning was Farm of the Spectre or Apparition. Just before the end of this road, King Orry's Grave is reached.

Turn right here and you are once again back on the A2. At Laxey, turn right and cross over the tram lines into Dumbell's Terrace, known to the locals as Ham and Egg Terrace, and park the car. Looking up the valley, your gaze rests upon the largest working water wheel in the world, Lady Isabella. For the less energetic or the elderly, you can in fact carry on up the valley to a car park which is adjacent to the Wheel.

The final leg of your journey takes you from Laxey along the A2 to just South of Baldrine village where you veer left after the tram level crossing lights onto the A11, Groudle Road. It is worth noting that trams do travel in both directions and the unwary motorist can be caught out at this crossing. Passing through Groudle you may catch sight of the popular Groudle miniature railway as it chugs around the headland. Soon the road grants you a fine view of Douglas Bay and then Port Jack is in sight.

Sheadings and Parishes

Dipping into the past always produces interesting facts and the Isle of Man is no exception. Proud to be the home of the oldest continuous Parliament in the world, the Island has many political differences from the adjacent countries. For instance there are no counties, instead ever since at least the 12th century, the Island was for administrative and political purposes traditionally divided into six sheadings. These Sheadings still exist to this very day and the derivation of the word is from the Gaelic *Seden* or, in more simplified form, six. Sheading is one of the few words still left in every day use from pre-Viking days. In modern times, the Sheadings still have a political purpose with, for example, Rushen being represented by three members of the House of Keys.

The Isle of Man was divided ecclesiastically into seventeen parishes, each of which takes its name from a patron saint. Two parishes which at first glance do not conform to this are Jurby and Ballaugh. Further study of the subject shows that these names have been contracted from Kirk Patrick of Jurby and Kirk Mary of Ballaugh. Similarly Rushen and Lezayre are derived as shortened versions of Kirk Christ Rushen and Kirk Christ Lezayre. There is an argument that proclaims Rushen is named after St. Russin, one of the twelve Missionary Fathers who, along with St. Columba, settled on the Island in the year 543 AD.

The six sheadings and their seventeen parishes are named as:

Ayre – Bride, Andreas and Lezayre.
Michael – Michael, Ballaugh and Jurby.
Glenfaba – Patrick, German and Marown.
Garff – Maughold and Lonan.

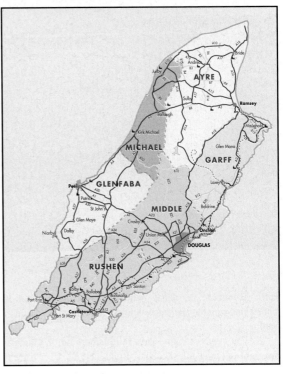

Middle – Onchan, Braddan and Santon.
Rushen – Rushen, Arbory and Malew.

For centuries now the sheadings have been drawn together, in a political sense, at the village of St. John's. Here stands the ancient Tynwald Hill or as it is called in Manx *Cronk Keeill Eoin* – Hill of St. John's Church. Legend tells us that the hill contains earth from all the seventeen ancient parishes, which would be in accordance with a known Norse practice. There is evidence to suggest that the site was the centre for tribal gatherings and the proclamation of new rulers, well before the system of sheadings and parishes was introduced to the Isle of Man.

Travelling to the Isle of Man

Most people travelling to the Isle of Man treat the journey as the start of their holiday and approach it with a sense of adventure. After all visiting an island is not just a case of jumping into a car, finding the nearest convenient motorway and hoping for a trouble free drive. Islands by their very nature are isolated and it is this very isolation that in the past kept the Romans from finding us and the Normans from conquering us. The very fact that there is a sea to cross has probably helped Ellan Vannin to preserve its peerless character and its unique atmosphere.

The gateways that serve the Island now means that travelling to our shores has become inevitably easier for the visitor. Connecting services by road and rail to the gateways has improved beyond recognition. Up to date information on all air and sea services can be obtained by contacting the various carriers direct or your local travel agent. As a useful tip, please note carefully important information such as check in times for air and sea journeys, and you should also allow plenty of time to get safely to your chosen gateway. If you can, please try and book early, there are certain periods in the year when the Island is extremely busy and advanced booking is the only sure way of ensuring you get tickets for the journey of your choice.

The Isle of Man is fortunate in the way in which the two main carriers, the Isle of Man Steam Packet Company and Manx Airlines promote the Island. Much effort is expended by their staff in ensuring that the message of the attractiveness of the Isle of Man as a holiday destination is carried far and wide. The Isle of Man Steam Packet Company operates a modern fleet of vessels and although founded in 1830, the company is still fiercely independent. During the summer months the sailings operate from six UK and Irish ports with the main all year round UK port being Heysham. Additionally during the season in association with Caledonian Macbrayne a service

is operated between Ardrossan and Douglas. Each of these gateways is served by good road and often by rail/bus connections, offering opportunities to reach the Island travelling as individuals, in family parties or in small to large groups. The Steam Packets' full booking facilities with British Rail which offer competitively priced fares from your local railway station and if you are travelling in a group of ten or more by rail/sea or just by sea, ask for details of their special group fares. In 1996 the Company will be operating the *King Orry* and the *Lady of Mann*. Each vessel on the service is equipped with all the facilities and comforts you would expect to find on a modern ferry and the Company is committed to offering you a first class service. There are on-board shopping facilities offering a range of goods including daily papers, confectionery, games, souvenirs and much more. Travellers from the Republic of Ireland have the benefit of Duty Free shopping. Eating is no problem on board and a range of tasty foods and beverages is available on all vessels.

Travelling to the Isle of Man by air has never been easier with Manx Airlines operating direct services from no less than thirteen UK and Irish gateways. Additionally there are a number of other hub airports throughout the British Isles and Europe which offer onward connections to the Island through British Airways Express with whom "Manx" have a strong connection.

Established in November 1982, Manx Airlines soon proved that it could provide a complimentary service to the sea carrier and although in direct competition, both companies do work together for the benefit of the Isle of Man. The modern fleet of aircraft, including British Aerospace 146 jets, British Aerospace ATPs (Advanced Turboprop), Shorts SD – 360s and British Aerospace Jetstreams ensure their passengers are carried in comfort and speed to the Island. The distinctive livery of the aircraft ensures that they are easily recognised and

All aboard to start your holiday.

WITH TWO SUPERBLY EQUIPPED SHIPS OPERATING TO
THE ISLE OF MAN, WHEN YOU TRAVEL WITH THE STEAM PACKET YOUR
HOLIDAY BEGINS THE MOMENT YOU STEP ABOARD.

BOTH OUR FLAGSHIP 'KING ORRY' AND THE
'LADY OF MANN' BOAST FIRST CLASS ONBOARD FACILITIES.
YOU CAN RELAX IN OUR LOUNGES; ENJOY A TASTY MEAL OR
A DRINK IN OUR CAFETERIAS AND BARS; BROWSE ROUND
OUR WELL-STOCKED SHOPS; OR EVEN TAKE IN ONE OF THE LATEST
FILMS IN OUR CINEMAS - WE'VE EVEN THOUGHT OF THE KIDS,
BY PROVIDING CHILDREN'S PLAY AREAS!

OUR 'FIRST CLASS' SERVICE TO MAN ON BOARD 'KING ORRY' WAS
RECENTLY RECOGNISED BY THE LES ROUTIERS ORGANISATION - WHEN
THE STEAM PACKET BECAME THE FIRST PASSENGER FERRY SERVICE IN
THE WORLD TO EARN A RECOMMENDATION OF EXCELLENCE!

SO IF YOU'RE TRAVELLING TO THE ISLE OF MAN,
THERE'S NOTHING QUITE LIKE TRAVELLING WITH THE STEAM PACKET -
BECAUSE IT'S ALL ABOARD TO GET YOUR HOLIDAY OFF TO A
WONDERFULLY RELAXING START!

TEL: 01624 661661

A first class service to Man

I.O.M. STEAM PACKET CO. LTD., DOUGLAS, ISLE OF MAN IM99 1AF.

the strong affinity with all things Manx is emphasised by the national motif on the tail, and the words *Skianyn Vannin*, Wings of Man, near the front of the aircraft.

Manx Airlines have always worked hard to involve package holiday operators in their plans and if you require this type of holiday there are a number of ways of achieving it. Elsewhere in the guide are adverts from local package holiday operators and it is suggested that contact with one or other of them is the best way of getting up to date information. None of the flights take any great length of time to bring the happy tourist here. If you can't wait until your first meal on the Isle of Man, enjoy the very good free in-flight meal or snack. Group travel is available with "Manx" and they love to carry golfers over to play the excellent courses, but be sure that you let them know in good time to help them make the appropriate arrangements for your clubs. If you are flying from Manchester and travelling out from the city centre,

the new rail link certainly helps Manx Airlines passengers make the right connection.

Geographically the Island is ideally situated to receive visitors from the closer parts of the British Isles but increasingly, we are being discovered by tourists from further afield and all parts of the globe. To assist in planning your journey to the Isle of Man an indication of travel distances and times from the gateways is provided.

Sea journey distance in miles (crossing times in hours and minutes) to the Isle of Man: Ardrossan 106 (8.00) Dublin 82 (5.00) Fleetwood 56 (3.20) Belfast 79 (4.45) Heysham 59 (3.45) Liverpool 73 (4.30)

Flight distance in miles and time (in minutes) are for direct travel to the Isle of Man: Belfast 62 (30) Leeds/Bradford 122 (55) Birmingham 162 (60) Liverpool 88 (30) Blackpool 68 (30) London Heathrow 251 (60) Cardiff 193 (60) Luton 234 (70) Dublin 79 (30) Manchester 108 (40) Glasgow 124 (50) Newcastle 133 (60) Jersey 352 (135)

Travelling around the Isle of Man

As the title suggests, this section of the guide deals with the internal transport system of the Isle of Man or you could walk! Nowhere on the Island is geographically more than five and a half miles from the sea and the many roads and tracks criss-crossing the countryside soon bring you back to the coast. The walkers amongst the readers may well be interested to learn that the Manxman calls his walking-stick *Bock-Yaun-Fannee*, John the Flayer's Pony. So named because John was said to have flayed his poor beast and to have as a consequence been obliged to travel on foot.

There are good maps of the Isle of Man available and if you are a keen rambler then a good buy is the Isle of Man Public Rights of Way Map, which is published by the Isle of Man Department of Highways, Ports and Properties. The OS Map has been mentioned elsewhere in the

publication and is an excellent guide to people as they move around the Island. The Island measures at its extremities 33 miles (52kms) by 13 miles (22kms) and with a total land mass area of some 227 square miles (572 sq.kms) there is a large area to explore.

Horse Trams

Disembarking from the ferry at Douglas, you are transported back into a bygone age. In transport terms the Isle of Man lies in a time warp, where even the surrounding Irish Sea seems little changed. Life is much as we imagined it was on the adjacent islands decades ago. Running the length of the Douglas Promenades, in front of the brightly painted hotels and guesthouses, the echoing clip-clop of the horse trams immediately relaxes the tourists and is a reminder of pre-motor vehicle days. Dating from 1876, the horse trams offer a leisurely trot between the Jubilee Clock to the Strathallan Terminus at Summerland. There are numerous tram stops, but please take care when boarding or alighting from the trams ... and do pay attention to the instructions from the conductors. The open air trams are known as "toast racks", look at the first one you see and you will understand why! Don't worry about the horses, all 40 plus animals are specially trained for the traffic and the track is so designed that a man can actually pull, with ease, a fully laden tram along the full length of the route. The working conditions are good with short days – a two hour shift per day in the season and all winter off to enjoy the grazing – and that just for the horses!

Douglas Corporation operates a pension scheme for these delightful beasts of burden and when the time comes to retire, a permanent home awaits them at the Isle of Man Home of Rest for Old Horses. If you love horses take a trip out to the Home of Rest on Richmond Hill, it's on the bus route to Castletown with a stop right outside and there is ample parking for cars by the stables. Take care here when turning or crossing the road because the premises are on a fast stretch of main road. A firm favourite with all, the amenities here include a cafe, gift shop, a small museum, facilities for the disabled ... and admission is free. The horses love to see the visitors and usually respond when called by name.

Electric Trams

Strathallan Terminus at the North end of the bay, houses the rolling stock and provides workshop facilities for the Manx Electric Railway. In 1993 the MER celebrated its centenary. These are no replicas but the original rolling stock from the 1890s, and passengers are offered a genuine opportunity to step back in time and experience this working "time capsule". If you are fortunate you may be on board one of two of the oldest working tramcars still in use anywhere in the world, and travel to Ramsey along the twisting and turning seventeen and a half mile route to Ramsey via the important railhead in the village of Laxey.

There you will find the only mixed gauge railway junction in the British Isles from where you can switch to the Snaefell Mountain Railway, the only electrically worked mountain railway still operating in the British Isles and 100 years old in 1995 .

Mountain Railway

Change systems at Laxey for the four mile climb to the summit of the Island's highest point ... it's a must for all visitors. The slow and gradual ascent up the side of Laxey Glen provides bird's eye views of the famous Laxey Wheel, restored and acting as a reminder that not so many decades ago Laxey was a centre for lead and zinc mining. After crossing the TT Course, the trams pause for a short while at the Bungalow Station before tackling the final stretch to the summit of Snaefell – in Manx *Sniaul* and *Snoefjall* from the Scandinavian meaning Snow Mountain. The Summit Station and cafe is the work place of the "highest paid person" on the Island. A short walk brings you to the mountain's peak. Catch your breath and take in the seven Kingdoms, the trip is worth it just for that view alone. After enjoying such inspiring views, the return journey awaits. Descending the mountain can leave you almost with a sense of loss. In no time at all the Snaefell tram is soon passing above the outlying houses and Dumbell's Terrace – former homes of the brave miners.

From Laxey, many tourists retrace their journey to Douglas past pretty little stations rejoicing in wonderful names such as Fairy Cottage, Ballabeg, Baldrine, Groudle Glen and Onchan. Others head North via the stations of Cornaa, Ballajora and Dreemskerry to Ramsey. To commemorate the MER's centenary a new visitor centre has been opened at the northern terminus. Open during the season it is dedicated to the fascinating history of the railway. Ramsey played its part in the building of the Mountain Railway, for it was from there that in 1895 the ten year old steam engine "Caledonia" was sent by sea to Laxey. After careening the vessel in Laxey harbour the engine was moved on baulks and rollers through the village to the station to assist in the construction of the new railway. What a feat the building of the railway must have been and what a contribution from the "Caledonia". Steaming up and down the mountain daily without the benefit of fell brakes this, the heaviest engine in Manx railway history, did the job on the hand and steam brakes alone. This famous old engine repeated the feat on a number of occasions in 1995 as part of the Mountain Railways' centenary celebrations.

Steam Trains

In June 1872 on the waste land of South Douglas known locally as "The Lake", a gang of navvies began work on what was to become a railway terminus. At the top end of Douglas inner harbour is a rather imposing red brick building now doing service as the Island's Customs and Excise Service headquarters but which originally was the headquarters of the Railway Company. The Isle of Man Steam Railway is one of the Island's unique institutions, protected by Government, the public and by a work force that has a fierce pride and a dedication much envied by larger systems elsewhere.

From Douglas Station the one hundred and twenty year old rolling stock carries you along through magnificent countryside to Port Erin in the far South of the Island, along sixteen miles of well maintained track. On past Ballasalla, historical Castletown and Port St Mary to the centre of the South West village of Port Erin, the track wends its busy way. There is usually time to have a look around the near vicinity of the railhead and if your hobby is trains, the Railway Museum is certainly worth a visit. The railway cafe is recommended for a cup of tea or some home made cakes or scones. The Station's waiting rooms are full of railway

Isle of Man Railways

memorabilia, evoking memories of another era, long lost to many places in the British Isles ... ah happy days!

The Douglas – Port Erin line is all that remains to remind the visitor of a network of steam railways which also took the traveller from the capital to Peel and Ramsey via the Island's central valley. The northern line branched off at St John's. Great was the excitement generated when the Peel and Ramsey trains left St John's Station simultaneously and appeared to race for the "right of track". In reality there were of course two tracks, but it used to amuse the passengers and was

a throw back to the days when two separate railway companies operated to Peel and Ramsey. From St John's, a railway line was laid up the glen to link Foxdale lead mines with the main line system. The ardent railway enthusiast will soon find that there were many more railways on the Island and there is a lot of fun to be had searching for old tracks and buildings.

1996 sees yet another railway milestone with the Groudle Glen railway celebrating its centenary. This 2-ft gauge line climbs up out of the lower reaches of the Glen and winds its way along the hillside through trees, gorse, bracken and heather

Laxey Station

to the clifftop terminus. The views are splendid and all the credit can be put down to the willing volunteers and supporters who have worked so hard to restore this marvellous little railway to its former glory. During centenary year there will be lots of extra attractions added but each year this special railway just seems to go rom strength to strength. Normally only operating a regular service in the summer months there are "specials" at other times of the year, check with the TIC for details.

Buses

Isle of Man Transport not only operates the railways but also provides an Island-wide bus service as part of an integrated bus and rail public transport network. Careful study of their timetables will show the tourist that bus times are usually carefully co-ordinated where possible with the trains and trams. The fun of roaming the countryside by bus is that one gets an opportunity to have a "skeet" over the hedge as you journey along.

Coaches

Privately owned coaches also operate on the Island. The most popular of the companies is Tours Isle of Man, offering morning, afternoon and evening mystery tours or full day round the Island tours as well as providing transfer services for package holidays from and to the Sea and Air Terminals. Their blue and white liveried vehicles depart from Douglas Promenade throughout the season and a trip out on one of their coaches is worthwhile. "Tours" drivers have an encyclopaedic knowledge of the Isle of Man and are always glad to lend a helping hand when needed. Not content with driving around the Island, they also operate a comprehensive holiday tour programme to the UK, Ireland and Europe, so there is a lot of experience behind the wheel and in dealing with the travelling public. Always to the front with new ideas, they can now lay claim to being the first Manx based tour operator to use successfully the Channel Tunnel.

Car Rental

Car Rental vehicles are an extremely popular means of getting around the Island. There are a number of reputable companies offering the full range of vehicles for hire, from small four seaters to minibuses (with all seats belted). Mylchreests and Empire Garage come highly recommended.

Jules Verne

The Isle of Man's unique transport system allows the visitor to travel easily around the Island. For many people it is the main reason for visiting, others see it as an unexpected bonus but whatever the reason this is no modern day replica of how things used to be. The engines, trams and rolling stock are the originals! They have survived in their original form largely because as a small island without a huge supporting population, they had to last. There never ever was going to be a modernisation or replacement programme, simply because the money was never available and they survived until such time when it was realised that these Victorian modes of transport remained, unharmed by the progress of the twentieth century. The Island's transport system appeals to all ages. It is the means of travelling back to the past without leaving the present; how Jules Verne would have envied us, even if the travel is to the past and not the future! The Isle of Man can offer the visitor an opportunity to leave behind the cares and worries of the modern world even if only for a short while.

Walking & Leisure Activities

Walking

Port St Mary to Port Erin

These walks are geared to people touring the Island by car who enjoy walking and who would like to sample a little of what the Island has to offer to the walker in the way of beauty and variety. The hikes are spread around the Island and based on principal towns and villages and choice is given for both medium and short walks with an indication given as to their extent or difficulty.

You will almost certainly find yourself in either Port Erin or Port St Mary during your travels so what better place to start. Try a sample section of the Coastal Footpath which is known as *Raad ny Foillan*, The Road of the Gull and you will see the symbol of a gull on waymarkers which give the direction of the path.

Start from Port St Mary and the car park by the Point Hotel which is near the landward end of the Breakwater. The full walk covers a distance of approximately 7 miles and you should allow 5 hours. The walk is strenuous but not difficult; for those who feel that may be too far, then a diversion can be made which will embrace Cregneash village and will take approximately 2 hours.

Leaving your car near the outer harbour, walk along the path by the sea wall heading South passing a lime kiln now used as a shelter, soon returning to the promenade which you must follow to the end. Now follow the path on the cliff side of the concrete boundary wall to the golf course. It is quite safe and commands good views over Perwick and the coast over which we shall walk. Soon the path passes through an iron wicket gate and then skirts the grounds of what used to be the Perwick Bay Hotel. After a short distance we shall join the public road, turning left and following through Perwick up a steep climb to join the road from Glenchass. Carry straight on along the very narrow surfaced road above Perwick Bay for about half a mile. At the end of the surfaced road, cross the stile by the gate and continue along the track through several fields. When the track finishes, continue across the last field veering slightly left to a hole in the wall. As you pass through the wall, strike up to the right and head across the open headland for the stile, taking care to avoid the cliff edge.

Through the stile there is a little scrambling to get up to the wall which you will follow all the way to the top. This is the steepest part of the walk and be sure to stay near the wall as it is easier. Stop for a breather and look down at Sugar Loaf rock with its colonies of Kittiwake, Fulmar and Guillemots. You will also be able to admire the view across Bay Stakka and the Chasms. The path brings you to the Chasms which is a natural phenomena of fissures in the cliff and you will have to step across one of the chasms. It is not difficult but it requires care, particularly if you have no head for heights. Aim for the old building and go through the gate and follow the wall to the left a short distance to a stile. If you are taking the short walk, you will take a different route from here.

Over the wall and all you have to do is follow the path and admire the view. Look back as you start to descend above Bay Stakka and you will again have a good view of the Chasms and Sugar Loaf. The path crosses a stream and then starts to climb over the back of Spanish Head. If you have children with you, please take care because sections of the cliff path are exposed. Soon the path rounds the corner above Spanish Head and you will see the whole of the Calf of Man across the Sound with the small island of Kitterland between it and the mainland. At the right time of year and

Coastal Path

more especially at low water you may be able to hear the seals crying on the rocks of the Calf.

The track climbs to the top of Cronk Mooar before dropping steeply down towards Burroo Ned which you will see below you. Cross another stream on a wooden bridge before climbing round the back of Buroo Ned from which you will be able to see Spanish Head across *Baie ny Breechyn*, The Bay of the Breeches. The path soon joins the green adjoining the Sound Cafe, a perfect place to stop for refreshment. Continue along the green passing the Thousla Cross to the stile. Once over the stile you are back on the Coastal Path which you will follow all the way to Port Erin. The path starts to climb and you overlook *Aldrick*, The Bay of the Old People. As you turn above the bay, the path swings below an unusual rock formation known locally as Jacob's Rock. The stiff climb continues until you emerge above Bay Fine and commands a fine view over the bay to Bradda Head and Port Erin in the background.

Follow the promenade to its junction with Strand Road and turn right up the hill and then left

to Station Road. If you haven't visited the Railway Museum now is your chance and you could take the train the short journey to Port St Mary. Otherwise follow Station Road out of the village as far as the roundabout at the Four Roads and turn right passing the station to walk into Port St Mary and return to your car.

If you are taking the short walk then you must go through the gate at the Chasms and follow the path straight up the hill to the brown hut on the skyline. Cross the stile and follow the surfaced road down to Cregneash Village. Make time to look at the buildings which are maintained as a living museum and a tribute to the heritage of the Isle of Man. Join the main road by the green telephone kiosk above the church, turn right and follow the road down to Port St Mary. On the way you will have plenty of time to admire the panoramic view over the South of the Island. As you approach the village in Plantation Road take care to veer right along Cronk Road and the Lhargan to join High Street and return to where you left the car.

Peel

Moving on to Peel, here are two walks of similar length but much easier going. The longer walk is about 7 miles in length and can be walked in 3 hours or less, the shorter walk is almost half the distance.

Starting from the main town car park off Market Place, cross the road to St Peter's Church and down Castle Street to Crown Street, turn right and join the Promenade. Walk along the Promenade as far as the Creg Mallin Hotel and turn up Walpole Road. Half way up take the lane to the left and walk towards the headland. The path climbs beside a sandstone wall before opening up onto the headland proper above *Traie Fogog*, Periwinkle Shore, the views back over Peel and north towards Kirk Michael and the sand cliffs beyond to Jurby are worth stopping to admire.

Follow the path along the cliff top until it turns inland above *Cass Struan*, Stream Foot or End, with the red sandstone rocky shoreline of Caines Strand. The track joins the main road to Kirk Michael and you must turn left as you go through the gate. Follow the road for about quarter of a mile to the disused railway station at St German's halt. Take care as there are sections without a footpath. The station building is unmistakable and there is a description of the disused railway which is self explanatory.

We are going to follow the track bed of the old line off to the right towards St Johns. The line was originally built in 1879 by the Manx Northern Railway Co. to serve the north of the Island and later joined to the Isle of Man network serving the rest of the Island at St Johns. A number of bridges carrying minor roads over the railway are soon passed and then the old track bed runs steadily downhill to St Johns. *Knocksharry*, translated as McSharrey's Hill, is to the left with the wooded hillside above. See if you can spot the legendary giant's fingers. The former line runs through fairly open ground on glacial deposits interspersed with the occasional granite intrusion.

As you approach the Poortown Road overbridge the track bed curves to the left. Look up at the bank on the left and you will see the remains of an old stone wall and wooden sleepers. This was a raised loading bay for a horse tramway that brought stone from the nearby quarry and which is still the major source of granite roadstone for the Island. Pass under the bridge and the site of the former Poortown Halt, little more than the concrete base now remains. Straight ahead is the bulk of Slieau Whallian, to the left you will see Poortown Quarry and to the right the granite boss of *Cronk Lheannag*, Hill Meadow.

The railway used to cross the main Douglas to Peel highway on a bridge which has since been removed. The path drops down the side of the embankment on one side of the road and back up to the old trackbed on the other. Be careful crossing the road as traffic is very fast and drivers may not be expecting people to cross. The track now descends rapidly on a sweeping curve to run alongside the disused railway that once ran from Douglas to Peel. Take care walking here because you have to join the old track, now forming the Heritage Trail, and follow it to the right to Peel.

You are now in a western part of the central valley running alongside the river Neb. The track is generally in the open except for a short section in a cutting near *Ballawyllin*, Byllinge's Farm, which used to be a problem with snow when the railway was still running. After a short distance walking along the flood plain of the river, you will pass through some curragh land which will give you an insight into what most of this area was like when the railway was built.

A short distance after this swampy area look for the small timber footbridge carrying the path across the Glenfaba millrace. Notice that the formation widens here and if you look very carefully you will see an embankment running off through the trees on the South side of the trail. This is where a short branch was built during the 1914-18 war to a prisoner of war camp at Knockaloe about a mile away, which housed almost 20,000 prisoners.

Carry on and you will pass the mill on your right and the water wheel can still be seen under the bridge and here is the River Neb. The line entered Peel through a brickworks and kipper houses but the area is now an industrial site largely occupied by a new Electricity Power Station. Look for the sign showing the route of the Heritage Trail and follow it into Peel alongside the river. This is a much better entry to the town and when you reach the harbour bridge, follow Mill Road to the right alongside what used to be the old station yard now being developed as a Heritage Centre ("The House of Manannan"). Up Station Road and Market Place to return to your car. If you are taking the short walk then all you have to do is turn right at the Coast Road when you leave the headland path and return to Peel. Continue straight on all the way into Peel and through Michael Street turning right at the end into Market Place.

Ramsey

The next two walks are in the North of the Island and centred on Ramsey. The longer walk is a little over 6 miles and you should allow 3 hours and the shorter one is less than 3 miles but you should allow 2 hours.

Park in the main car park at Ramsey, off Station Road and near the Town Hall. Leave the car park and walk up Bowring Road over the bridge at the top of the harbour. Admire some of the grand buildings which reflect the past wealth of Ramsey in Victorian times. Carry on up the hill passing the Grove Rural Life Museum on the left which is definitely worth a half day visit. Now you are entering the rich northern plain which has probably the most fertile farmland in the Island. Pass the Grest elderly persons home until you come to the disused Dhoor School which is on your left opposite the prominent castellated tower of Boliviamount which can be seen through the trees.

Look for the Right of Way sign on the left and

Injebreck Reservoir

129

turn down the grassy lane and follow the path through farmland until you come to the Jurby Road just on the edge of Ramsey. The path crosses the dried basin of an area once occupied by one of several shallow glacial lakes formed in the flood plain as the ice cap retreated from the Island at the end of the Ice Age. Turn right at the road and follow it for half a mile passing what used to be the Cronk Raugh Sanatorium. At the next junction turn left and follow the road to the Garey. The views ahead of you are of the northern hills dominated by Snaefell. Again look out for the Right of Way signs where the railway used to cross the road. You must take the path on the left along the wide track heading for *Ballakillingan*, Farm of St Fingan's Church.

The track soon joins the Sulby River which you cross by a footbridge. This river is still the largest in the Island but is no longer the turbulent force that it used to be having been tamed by a reservoir constructed in its upper reaches which now serves the whole of the Island. The Right of Way is now reduced to a path through farmland and ahead you will see Lezayre Parish Church nestling in the trees. At the farm the path bears right and then follows the farm street to the main Ramsey to Kirk Michael Road, turn left and walk along the road until you are opposite the war memorial.

Cross the road and walk a little distance up the road round the back of the church. Look for the farm gate on the left and go through it heading for the plantation. At the second gate entering the plantation, stop and look back at the church before climbing through the plantation for a quarter of a mile. Following the rather poorly defined track through the trees and you will soon join a surfaced track by a gate. Don't go through the gate, instead turn left and follow the track downhill all the way back to the road. The track rounds the bluff of Sky Hill and you will pass a commemorative plaque which marks the site of a battle between the Manx and the Norse in 1079 AD which led to the surrender of the Isle to Viking rule.

Join the road again and turn right for quarter of a mile then right again into the *Glen Auldyn Road*, Swan's Glen. After another quarter of a mile

look for the Right of Way sign on the left to *Claghbane*, sometimes this word is split as in *Clagh bane*, either which way it means White Stone, and the Hairpin Corner. Follow this path which skirts Milntown and then passes through a pleasant rural setting on the edge of Ramsey with Ramsey Golf Club on the left and a fascinating ridge of low hills on the right. The path joins the Snaefell Mountain Road at the Hairpin Corner which is one of the best known corners on the world famous T.T. Course. Walk down the road into Ramsey and return to your car.

For the short walk, which is quite strenuous, leave the car park and head for the Hairpin Corner on the T.T. Course. Into Parliament Square, past the bus station and up May Hill retracing the last section of the long walk.

At the Hairpin look for the Right of Way sign on the right hand side of the road that will take you up the side of Elfin Glen. The path is well defined and fairly steep. As it swings away from the glen and continues up into the trees, look for a gate on the left clearly marked to the Albert Tower. Go through and head for the tree lined stony crag and go through a second metal gate following the main path and the right fork a little distance from the gate. Follow the path until you come to a shelter, turn sharp right and follow the path to the Tower. The descriptive plaque above the door tells you why it is so named and if you stop to admire the view, you will see why Prince Albert came here.

Having climbed all the way up here, there is only one thing for it. Yes, you guessed correctly, it's all the way back down again. Go back to the path beside the shelter and follow it to the main road. Cross over and walk a little way up the road and take the path to the left down the steps on towards Ballure Road through Lhergy Frissell. Turn right at the road and walk alongside the tram track to the main road, turn left and follow it into Ramsey along Waterloo Road and the car park.

Douglas

The last walk giving you a taste of what the Island has to offer covers the east of the Island and is centred on Douglas. The walk is 6 miles long and you should allow a leisurely 3 hours to do it in.

Start at the Shaws Brow car park in the centre of Douglas near to the recently renovated Town Hall. Leave by the exit into Athol Street which is the business centre of the town and turn left towards the ornate clock tower which forms part of the elaborate station buildings of the Isle of Man Railway. Cross the road and walk down Bank Hill onto the quay and over the Douglas Bridge at the top of the harbour. You must now turn right and follow the Old Castletown Road out of Douglas alongside the river from which the town takes its name. It is often possible to see swans, ducks and moorhen on the river banks.

As you approach the castellated gateway to the Nunnery follow the path to the right which skirts the grounds and follows the course of the river. Pass under the steam railway bridge and follow the path until it reaches a stile and crosses a stream. Turn left and follow the path alongside this stream which is the Middle River. You are now also on the edge of the Municipal Golf Course at Pulrose and almost out of Douglas. The path eventually joins the main road to Castletown at

Kewaigue where you must turn right and walk up the hill for about a quarter of a mile. At Middle Farm turn left and follow the farm track to Port Soderick. You really are in the country now and yet still very close to Douglas.

As you approach Port Soderick village the path becomes much narrower and suddenly you are on the Old Castletown Road once again. Turn right and follow the road to the next junction where you must take the road down the hill leading towards the station. Walk under the bridge to emerge above the Port Soderick Glen and follow the road round to the left and on to the Marine Drive.

Now all you have to do is follow the Marine Drive back along the route of the former Douglas Southern Electric Tramways towards Douglas. Pause awhile on Douglas Head, the views are spectacular.

Leisure Activities

With over 200 different events and attractions taking place on the Island during the year there is a wide choice... something for everyone in fact.

Holidays are the time to try new activities and on the Island there is scope for new sports to be tackled. If you have never been clay shooting a visit to the Country Gun Club at Upper Ballagick, Santon will probably whet your appetite. John Quilliam is a very skillful and friendly coach and in next to no time he will have you recognising clays called high pheasant, which flies up and away from you, bolting rabbits bouncing unexpectedly along the grass and a springing teal that explodes upwards like a Mount Vesuvius. Clay shooting is an ideal family sport and the special low recoil cartridges and small stocked shotguns means that the ladies and youngsters can compete on equal terms with Dad. Ballagick is easy to find. Drive out of Douglas on the main Castletown Road A5 and just past the Mount Murray make a right turn on to the B37 or if you miss that turn there is another to your right, a little way down the road just before the Lancashire Hotel ... and follow the signs.

Museums of Mann

Manx National Heritage

T he early days of the Isle of Man are briefly described elsewhere within this publication, but for the visitor with more than a little passing interest in the Island and its rich history, The Story of Mann really begins with Manx National Heritage, *Eiraght Ashoonagh Vannin*.

Over the centuries the history of Mann has been likened to a tapestry, with people and events drawn together as if colourful threads, creating an image of island life as it was for our forefathers. It is a history that tells of great tragedies, great happenings, arts, crafts ... and also periods of great happiness. The first-time visitor to our shores soon discerns that history lies around almost every corner and the skillful manner in which Manx National Heritage interprets this tapestry ensures that locals and tourists alike are aware of the value of the past.

The secret of Manx National Heritage's success has been to treat all the heritage sites and the landscape as equals, binding them all together as it were, as one. This innovative idea was rewarded by their being acknowledged as the British Isles Museum of the Year 1992/93, European Museum of the Year 1993 Special Award, both of which followed on from the Gulbenkian Museum and Gallery Awards 1992 for Most Improved Catering Facilities. Future planned developments will ensure that the Isle of Man and its heritage will continue to enrich the life of the Island and maintain the lead that the Heritage team give to the adjacent islands and elsewhere. As part of the "Story of Mann" strategy for heritage co-ordination throughout the Island, Manx National Heritage have commissioned a multi-million pound project which will link together under one roof an interpretation of Peel, Peel Castle and Odin's Raven. To be known as "The House of Manannan" work commenced on this exciting development in 1995 and will, when completed, provide the Island and its visitors with another wonderful heritage asset.

You are invited to turn the pages of our history by visiting as many of the sites as possible. The Museum in Douglas is the hub of the many spokes that make up and tell the Story of Mann and whilst the manner of the interpretation is comprehensive, there is no substitution for a visit to the many sites of archaeological and historical importance that abound. There are a number of very good leaflets which give guidance to the various locations and the highly visible road signs ensure that directions are easily followed. If you need a snack, a number of the heritage sites have facilities to cater for most tastes and parking is easy, just leave your car in the Chester Street multi-storey car park and cross over directly to the Museum via the new link bridge from the top deck. The Heritage Shops found in the Museum and at each of the Story of Mann sites (during the summer season) offer a remarkable range of quality goods; ideal for practical gifts and souvenirs of your visit.

Forts, Chapels, Crosses and Castles

Contained within the Island's 227 square miles are prehistoric monuments, Iron Age hill forts, early Christian chapels, Norse houses, collections of ancient crosses and the outstanding Peel and Rushen castles. Moving to more modern eras, there is Tynwald Hill, Cregneash Village, Laxey Wheel, the Nautical Museum, the Grove Museum and much more to visit. All have one thing in common – they blend in with their natural surroundings. Under the Manx National Heritage umbrella, which is well supported by a number of voluntary groups, lies responsibility for the preservation of the Manx countryside. Building developments are required to be sympathetic to the area and the Island as a whole. The extensive land holdings of

The Story of Mann

All the family will enjoy travelling back through 10,000 years of fascinating and sometimes turbulent Manx Heritage. This international award winning story is portrayed at **eight** major attractions throughout the Island.

EUROPEAN MUSEUM OF THE YEAR

MUSEUM OF THE YEAR 1992–1993
THE HIGHEST MUSEUM AWARD IN THE BRITISH ISLES

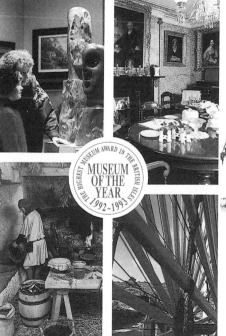

The Story of Mann

Collect your **FREE** 28 page booklet at any Tourist Information Office, Heritage Site or Hotel Reception.

Manx National Heritage

Eiraght Ashoonagh Vannin

Manx National Heritage, The Manx Museum, Douglas, I.O.M. 01624 675522

FARMERS AND CROFTERS | CELTIC ISLANDERS AND VIKING INVADERS
KINGS AND LORDS OF MANN | LAXEY MINERS | SHIPS AND THE SEA

the Manx Museum and National Trust and the Manx Nature Conservation Trust ensure that natural beauty spots are left undisturbed for the enjoyment of the generations to come. The Manx Nature Conservation Trust actively encourages the visitor to sample the delights of the unspoilt countryside and this is supplemented by Visitor Centres and Nature Trails found in various parts of the Island such as at Scarlett, The Ayres and the Tynwald Craft Centre.

Travelling around the Island without a car is easy by using the various forms of public transport e.g. the steam and electric railways – working museum pieces in their own right – buses and coaches. Timetables are readily available or ring 663366/ 662525 for up to date travel information. A car is recommended though because some of the smaller heritage sites are off the beaten track.

The Manx Museum

Without doubt the best place to acquaint yourself with what Manx National Heritage has to offer is to begin by visiting the Manx Museum in Douglas. If you are on foot, head for St Thomas's Church and the Museum lies just behind it, at the top of Crellins Hill. Should you be driving to the Museum there are usually plenty of parking spaces in the Chester Street car park, which is connected to the Museum by a footbridge. For those folk who have a handicapped person in their party, it is possible to pull up outside the main doors and discharge passengers but please note, parking and turning space is very restricted outside the Museum entrance.

The best advice available recommends our visitors start their journey into the past by viewing the magnificent "Story of Mann" film. The atmosphere generated by the film will, it is guaranteed, stay with you for the duration of your visit to the Island. Home to much of the Island's art treasures and artefacts, the Museum is not a place to be rushed. In fact there is no need to even leave it for refreshments as there is an excellent restaurant on site near the well-stocked heritage shop.

For the serious student of history, the modern

Manx Museum

research facilities offered by the Museum Library are excellent, particularly for delving into family trees. The Island was fortunate in that much of their written records were saved from the worst excesses of Henry VIII and the Reformation.

A helpful note for those visitors who are members of the National Trust, Scottish National Trust, English Heritage and certain overseas trusts, is that admission, on production of the appropriate documentation, is free to all those sites where a charge is normally made. Enjoy your visit to Manx National Heritage and all it has to offer.

Legends of Mann

Like many other small communities legends and stories grow up and are perhaps expanded as the years and generations pass by. The Isle of Man is no exception to this generalisation ... or is it? You see many of us happen to believe that all the myths, legends and stories handed down to us are true!

Manx place names, as you have seen in other

parts of this guide, are different from those in your own locality. The simple explanation could be that in days of yore English was not spoken here hence the lack of English place names and indeed the Manx had toget to grips with the language of the Norsemen. Maybe the landscapes changed, traditions altered or perhaps there was an event of great historical significance, whatever the explanation, there is often no logical reason why a particular place received its name.

What's in a Name?

Take the name of this fair Isle ... you the reader may have always believed its name to be just that, yet the inhabitants know it by several other names. At the time of Caesar in 54 BC the Romans knew it as Mona. A century later the Roman writer and administrator Pliny "The Elder" was calling the Island Monapia. One hundred years on, in 139 AD we find the famous Graeco-Egyptian mathematician and geographer Ptolemy, referring to it as Monaoeda. As the centuries rolled by, variations of the name surfaced but it is not until the time of the Irish Annals circa 1084-1496 AD that a more recognisable form of our nation's name was seen, Manann or Manand. The rough translation of the name means mountainous or hilly land. There is a school of thought that believes that Mann may have taken its name from Manannan, the Celtic Neptune, God of the Sea, but it is much more likely that he was named from the Island.

For a long time now the Manx have referred to their homeland as Ellan Vannin, though the visitor will still find reference about the Island, to Mann. Whatever your preference please enjoy exploring our Island.

The Three Legs of Man

The Manx national symbol has for many centuries been the Three Legs of Man. Arguments as to its exact origins have always proved inconclusive but it does seem to have been introduced to the Island at least as long ago as 1266 AD. Alexander III of Scotland adopted the symbol when the Isle of Man was ceded to

Scotland. Perhaps his family connections with the Mediterranean island of Sicily holds the answer. In that far off island much use is made of a very similar symbol with the difference being that the Manx legs are armoured, the Sicilian's being bare. Our motto is interesting, *Quocunque Jeceris Stabit*; Which ever way you throw me, I shall stand.

Snakes, Graynoges and Moddey Dhoos

If you love wild life then the Island can be paradise. There is a marvellous variety of bird life and the Calf of Man is a world renowned bird sanctuary but don't expect to find any squirrels, badgers or snakes. Snakes were allegedly banished by St Maughold when he was thrown from his horse.

Staying on the subject of animals, *Graynoge's* the Manx name for Hedgehogs, it means something causing horror, only came to the Island about 1800. The schooner *"Hooton"* of Garlieston was wrecked at Rue Point. Amongst the salvage was a box of hedgehogs and some of them made

Fairy Bridge

135

good their escape. In more modern times Wallabies broke free from the Curraghs Wild Life Park and are said to be enjoying "the goodlife" in the North of the Island. The most famous Manx animal resident is the Manx Cat. There are many and varied stories about how they lost their tails ... it might be fun for you to find this out for yourself!

In Peel Castle under the Keep is a guardroom and it was here that one of the most famous legends in Manx history is set. Each night a large black dog, the *Moddey Dhoo*, would come and lie down in front of the fire. Viewing this apparition by the light of flickering candles the soldiers soon became quite used to its presence although they treated it with the greatest of respect and would not stay in the room alone with it. One day a drunken soldier followed it out of the guardroom, when he returned he was a changed man, and despite much pleading from his friends as to what he had seen, died in great agony some three days later.

Witches

Dealing with more human creatures takes the visitor to the foot of *Slieau Whallian*, Aleyn's Mountain at St John's, overlooking Tynwald Hill. Tradition has it that in Viking times witches were punished here by being placed into spiked barrels and rolled down the steep slopes of the hill. There is also a tradition that tells of the nearby Curragh Glass, Green Marsh, where the accused were put into the water and if they sank were presumed innocent, some good that did them!

Keeills

Buildings of great age and size are relatively scarce on the Island but they do exist and there are fine examples to be seen in Peel and Rushen castles. Rushen Abbey still has a few buildings standing and there are the remains of over 150 *Keeills*, Churches, dating from the 6th and 7th centuries, dotted about the countryside. Whilst the Island escaped the worst excesses of the Reformation the old buildings acted as stone quarries and suffered accordingly. One building on the Island that is roofless and in good condition is

Grove Museum

St Trinians Church at Crosby. There has never been a roof on the building, despite three separate attempts to place one on it. Legend tells of a spirit like creature called a Buggane who frightened anybody who attempted to roof over the walls.

Near to St Trinian's, legend tells of the Curse of St Patrick, when a thorn ran through his foot as he was in the act of dedicating the Island's first church in 444 AD. His response was to curse the field where the thorn was growing and decree that no crops would grow on this field forever.

The Little People

On the A5 Douglas to Castletown Road just past Santon Station is the Fairy Bridge. Well sign= posted, no self respecting local passes over this bridge without a word of greeting to the "Little People". Try *Laa Mie*, Good Day, pronounced "lay my" and they will be pleased! The Little People are of course the good fairies.

Bugganes, Phynnodderrees and other Spirits

Manx mythology indicates that there were a number of supernatural beings in existence. The *Phynnodderree*, a Hairy Satyr features often in the legends and seems to have been kindly disposed towards men often using his great strength to their advantage. Warning of future events was given by the Night-man or *Dooiney-oie*. Another friendly spirit and the guardian of certain families was the *Lhiannan Shee*. On the down side was the *Buggane*, mentioned earlier and very much an evil spirit. The *Cabbyl-Ushtey* was a water-horse, sometimes confused with the *Glashtin*, a Goblin. There also appeared in stories a water-bull, known to the inhabitants of Mann as the *Tarroo-Ushtey*. Much of the legendary history of the Island is recorded in songs and ballads.

The Sea

The sea has always played an important part in the history of the Island and legends tell of an Irishman, one Buck Whalley who was driven from his native land. To retain his wealth he had to comply with the conditions of his Father's will which required him always to reside on Irish soil. No problem to this enterprising gentleman he simply shipped into the Island several cargoes of Emerald Isle soil and built his house on it. This, the Fort Anne, later became home to Sir William Hilary, founder of the RNLI. The site of this fine building was just above Douglas harbour on Head Road. But unfortunately it has in recent years been demolished.

One of the finest seamen the Island ever produced was Captain Quilliam of H.M.S. *Victory* fame, but even with his close connections to Nelson he couldn't have had a more direct relationship with the famous hero of Trafalgar than John Lace of Kerrodhoo, Bride. Lace claimed that the shot which fatally wounded the Admiral passed through his arm first. Poor John Lace lost his arm in the incident and later drowned in Ramsey Bay.

The North of the Island seems to have been a good breeding ground for seamen. Sir Baldwin Walker KCB, who was born at Port-e-Vullen, Maughold, managed careers in both the Royal and Turkish Navies. His name when sailing under Turkish colours was Yavir Pasha.

Long before Sir Baldwin's era, it was said that the *"Great Harry"* built by Henry VIII as the first warship to have guns in her holds, sailed too close to the Manx cliffs and swept several flocks of sheep into the sea with her bowsprit!

Give me a C, give me a Q, give me a K

A close examination of the Manx Telecom telephone directory reveals that many Manx surnames begin with C, Q, or K. Kerruish is a much respected name in the Island and the legend attached to its origins is fascinating. In the long ago, a ship was wrecked off Maughold and four of the crew were observed swimming for the shore. Because the swimmers were of an undetermined nationality and unable to communicate with the locals they became known as *Kiare Rooisht*, Four Naked. The swimmers settled in Maughold and the name Kerruish is still synonymous with the Sheading.

Giants

Stepping ashore again and visiting the Sulby River above Tholt-y-Will, we find a legend telling of a *Tarroo-Ushtey* who lived there. Great care was always taken when travelling in the area. Close by was an old watermill and it is said that every miller who went into this mill disappeared. At last one soul, perhaps braver than the rest decided to solve the mystery. On entering the mill he discovered that a giant had been coming down from the mountain and disposing of the millers. It was "suggested" to the miller by the giant that he would suffer the same fate, but our brave friend volunteered to make himself useful by baking a cake for the giant. Risking his neck, the cunning miller handed the giant a sieve and told him to fetch water for the kneading. Giants are considered to be dull-witted and as he kept repeating the phrase "As fast as I get it, it disappears", the miller made good his escape, the only man to live to tell the tale.

On the subject of giants the largest ever Manxman was James Arthur Caley of Sulby. His full height was seven feet eleven inches and he weighed

44 stones. Arthur lived a relatively short life dying at the age of 43, it is said as a consequence of poisoning by a jealous rival. A cast of one of his hands is on display at the Museum. There are many other legends told about the life and times of our ancestors, too numerous to relate in this modest publication.

As you explore the Island try and imagine the conditions under which the people lived. It is not too difficult to see how close they lived to nature and how easy it must have been to interpret certain deeds as phenomena's of one kind or another.

BLUE BADGE GUIDES

MANX REGISTERED GUIDE

TEL: 672431/686766

Nature in Mann

One of the first things you notice about the Isle of Man are the great numbers and variety of birds. Wheeling and plunging from the cliffs or simply singing their hearts out in a secluded glen each of these species seem to know that they live in a land where people appreciate wildlife and derive great pleasure from their presence. The list seems endless and varies from the Manx shearwater, peregrine falcons, hen harriers, razorbills, guillemots, kittiwakes, wildfowl, cormorants – the Manx know them as jinny divers – through all the normal types found in the countryside to the rare red-legged chough. This unusual member of the crow family is well protected and so to speak, has been taken under the wing of our National Airline as one of their charitable projects.

The serious bird watcher will be pleased to know that the Calf of Man is a World renowned bird sanctuary, with its own permanently staffed bird observatory. Between 1962 and 1990, nearly 100,000 birds representing 134 species were ringed by the hardworking wardens, and still the job goes on. Sharing the Calf with the birds are a flock of Manx Loghtan sheep and a colony of Atlantic Grey seals. If you can not make the journey out to the Calf, try Maughold Head, that's another breeding ground, or one or other of the western beaches for the seals.

Fortunately the hedgerows of the Island have not suffered from the barbarous acts perpetrated elsewhere and as a consequence they still afford protection to the birds, insects, wildflowers and plants that bring so much colour and decoration to our everyday lives. Indeed the Highways Division of the Isle of Man Department of Transport earn much in the way of plaudits for their policy of bulb planting along the roads and lanes. Wildlife enthusiasts and nature lovers are well catered for through such places as the Curraghs Wild Life Park, the Ayres and Scarlett Visitor Centres, near Bride and Castletown respectively, the Manx Museum, the Marine Interpretation Centre at Port Erin and a number of other nature reserves and wetlands managed by the Manx Nature Conservation Trust. If you get a chance call in at their shop at the Tynwald Craft Centre.

Further protection for our wildlife is offered by the many plantations spread throughout the Island. Long ago Tynwald decided that their Forestry Division should devote time, energy and money to a re-forestation programme. Careful consideration is given to the siting of new woods and the result has been a noticeable improvement to an already beautiful countryside. A programme also exists whereby landowners can work in conjunction with the Government and plant broadleaf trees. All actions which act in favour of Mother Nature and wildlife.

If you come to the Isle of Man expecting to see creatures such as foxes, snakes, badgers, woodpeckers, lizards and other familiar species native to the rest of the British Isles, you will be disappointed. It seems they retreated with the ice some 10,000 years ago. One creature that is peculiar to the Island of course is the famous Manx cat. One small animal who did manage the sea journey however was the humble hedgehog, called *Graynoge* in the Manx.

Accommodation & Eating Out

DOUGLAS, LAXEY & THE EAST

ARRANDALE HOTEL, 39 Hutchinson Square, Douglas, Isle of Man IM2 4HW. Three Crowns Commended hotel, situated in a quiet residential area of Douglas, overlooking floral gardens. Comfortable accommodation, high quality fresh food and a homely atmosphere. Unrestricted street parking. Bed and breakfast from £17. Tel: 674907

ASHTEAD, 9 Christian Road, Douglas. Family run guest house. Good food. Special diets on request. Heating in all bedrooms. Tea and coffee. No restrictions. Close to all amenities. Open all year. Come and make yourself at home. Write or ring Jean for details. Tariff B&B £11.00, BB&EM £15.00. Tel:01624 676790

BALLACHRINK FARM COTTAGES, Ballaragh Road, Laxey IM4 7PJ. Five luxury mews cottages in five acres of unspoilt countryside. Panoramic views over Laxey Bay and Hills. All cottages have gas central heating, television, clock radio and all essentials. Write or telephone Kate Bishop for brochure and tariff. Tel: 01624 862155, Fax: 01624 861554. See page 84

BALLAWYLLIN, East Baldwin, Braddan, Isle of Man. Ballawyllin is a delightful Georgian style country house set in 12 acres in the totally unspoilt Baldwin valley, yet within 5 miles of Douglas. Excellent walking country. Peace, quietness and warm welcome await you. 3 Crowns Commended. Non-smokers only. Tel: 01624 851462

BEACH HOTEL, Central Promenade, Douglas IM2 4LN. Friendly and welcoming sea front hotel. Ideally situated for beach and all amenities. Excellent A La Carte restaurant. Patio bar with panoramic views of bay. On main bus, coach and horse tram routes. Please write/phone for brochure. Tel: 01624 673561

CLIFTON HOLIDAY FLATS, Clifton, 9 Drury Terrace, Douglas, Isle of Man IM2 3HY. All flats fully self-contained. Two people low season £90, high season £120. Each flat has bedroom, living room, equipped kitchen, shower and toilet. Also flat for four people on request. Colour TV in all flats. Tel: 01624 674651

COMFORTABLE DETACHED COUNTRY BUNGALOW, large garden, splendid view to South Barrule. Well equipped for 5 persons. Three bedrooms, CH, pets welcome. Near golf course and leisure centre. 4 Key Approved. Tel: 01323 728786

CORNAA GUEST HOUSE, 46 Murray's Road, Douglas, Isle of Man IM2 3HW. Small family guest house in a quiet area, near promenade. Personal supervision, home cooking. TV lounge, tea/coffee facilities in rooms. Children welcome. Special rates B&B £13.50 BB&EM £16.50. Package holidays can be arranged. Tel: 01624 676927

CRONK-DHOO FARM, Greeba, Isle of Man IM4 2DX. Country farmhouse and converted barn full of character in beautiful secluded country overlooking the central valley. Sleeps 6 & 4. Properties equipped to high standard. C/heating. Linen provided. Private car parking. Lovely gardens, barbecue area. 6 miles Douglas, 3 miles Peel. Tel: 01624 851327

CUNARD HOTEL, 28/29 Loch Promenade, Douglas, IM1 2LY. Friendly family run Hotel with panoramic views of whole bay. Ideal location with full facilities. Renowned for its welcome, food, bar and service. Close to all transport. Write, phone or fax for free brochure to Mrs G A Quirk. Tel: 01624 676728   Fax: 01624 676728 Freephone: 0500 121274 Ext.5. See page 31

EDELWEISS HOTEL, Queens Promenade, Douglas, Isle of Man. Why not turn back and have another look at the Edelweiss with its very unique facilities. No steps into hotel. Lift. All rooms en-suite. No parking restrictions apply on Queens Promenade. Three Crowns Commended. Tel: 01624 675115. See page 33

EMPRESS HOTEL, Central Promenade. 5 Crowns, highly commended hotel conveniently situated. 102 luxurously ensuite rooms with all modern facilities. Health club. Entertainment. Open all the year. Tel 01624 661155. See page 30

EXCELSIOR HOTEL, Queens Promenade, Douglas, Isle of Man IM2 4NE. A warm and friendly welcome awaits you at the Excelsior Hotel. Ideally situated for beach, local amenities, coach tours, casino and various entertainments. The hotel has a choice menu daily with 50% en-suite bedrooms. Tel: 01624 675773

FENISCLIFFE GUESTHOUSE, 10 Woodville Terrace, Douglas IM2 4HB. A warm friendly guesthouse in a quiet sunny position. Panoramic views over Douglas Bay. Close to beach and shops. Central heating, radio/intercom, TV, tea making facilities in all rooms. Comfortable lounge. Non-smokers only. A touch of class at an affordable price (£13.00 pp). Tel: 01624 612844, Fax: 01624 628020, e-mail: IOMHOTEL@advsys.co.uk

THE GREAVES, Sunnycroft, Ramsey Road, Laxey IOM IM4 7PD. Peace, tranquility and magnificent panoramic views, yet situated in Laxey Village near electric tram station/bus stop and shops. Homely guest house, good home cooking using local home grown produce. E.M. optional. £7.00 Contact Mrs Patsy Quirk. Tel: 01624 861500

GLENESK, 47 Royal Avenue West, Onchan, Isle of Man IM3 1HE. Small quiet comfortable registered guest house lower Onchan overlooking Douglas Bay, adjacent Onchan Pleasure Park. All bedrooms have colour television, tea/coffee facilities. Comfortable residents lounge. Ideal base for walkers, golfers, railway enthusiasts. Reasonable rates. Tel: 01624 676993

GRAND VIEW, Loch Promenade, Douglas. Right on sea front, central for all amenities. Popular family run guest house. Satellite TV, baby listening, packed lunches etc. Inclusive holiday arrangements by sea and air. Free brochure on request from Mrs Carole Ferrara. Tel: 01624 621308/621307

139

GREEBA HOLIDAY FLATLETS, c/o 52 Victoria Road, Douglas IM2 4HQ. Holiday flatlets close to promenade and Villa Marina. Comfortable, clean and homely. Colour TV. Linen provided. From £80 for 2 people. Also, in Port Erin, lovely old cottage in quiet select area. Beautiful rural and sea views. For details Tel: 01624 676919/674877

HAMPTON MANOR, Port Soderick, Isle of Man. Modern Country House. B&B with full English breakfast, set in 3 acres of lovely gardens. Magnificent views, ample parking. 5 minutes to shore and local pub. Convenient to Douglas and Castletown. Warm welcome. Tel: 01624 621539

HILBERRY MANOR, Little Mill Road, Onchan IM4 5BE. Secluded Victorian country house, spacious colourful garden, glorious views. All rooms have private bathrooms. Family run, optional evening meal, using local and home-grown produce. Ample parking. 10 mins to Douglas by car. Central location. Tel/Fax: 01624 661660. See page 32

HOYSHOERN STUDIO APARTMENT, West Baldwin, Marown, Isle of Man IM4 5HD. Peace and tranquillity for 2 people in fully equipped, centrally heated, self-contained Studio Apartment. Panoramic views over unspoilt countryside and mountains. 10 km from Douglas. Open all year round. Please ask for brochure. Tel: 01624 852716

IMPERIAL HOTEL, Central Promenade, Douglas. Ideally situated, family run hotel. 63 comfortable bedrooms, many en-suite, with TV, heating, tea/coffee facilities, intercom & radio. 2 Lifts. Entertainment and dancing. Tel 621656. See Page 31

KERROWGARROW FARM, Greeba, Nr St Johns, Douglas IM4 3LQ. Stay at Kerrowgarrow Farm in the heart of the Manx countryside, either bed and breakfast in the house or self-catering in a beautifully converted stone barn that sleeps 4-6 people. Walks arranged for naturalists. Tel: 801871

MAYFAIR HOTEL, 23 Loch Promenade, Douglas, Isle of Man. Centrally situated on promenade with panoramic views of bay and gardens. Close to shops, entertainment, and transport routes. Specialising in sports groups. A warm welcome all year round. For details contact John or Pauline Tel: 676968

MAXWELL HOUSE, 7 Stanley View, Broadway, Douglas. Small but with a touch of class. 3 Crown Commended. All en-suite. Colour TVs, satellite channels in all rooms. Private parking, licensed bar, discounts for sports groups, OAPs and family rooms. All inclusive holidays arranged. Tel: 01624 673069

MERRIDALE GUEST HOUSE, 30 Castlemona Avenue, Douglas. Small and friendly offering warm welcome. Rooms are standard, clean and comfortable, all have heating and tea/coffee making facilities. Guests TV lounge. Arrive as a guest, leave as a friend. Tel: 01624 673040

MILLBROOK HOTEL, 4 Drury Terrace, Broadway, Douglas. This comfortable refurbished hotel is situated within a few minutes walk of the promenade, parks and transport systems. Catering for family, sporting holidays and business interests. Good food, warm welcome. Contact Wendy Brennan for details. Tel: 01624 675699

MIRAMAR, 11 Empress Drive, Douglas. Look no further for self-contained holiday flats - Miramar is in the centre of the action. Only two minutes walk to the beach, close to all amenities. Free food starter pack. Special offers available. Write/phone Pat Keenan for brochure. Tel: 01624 624474

MOUNT MURRAY HOTEL AND COUNTRY CLUB, Santon. The Isle of Man's Premier and only four star Hotel with wonderful facilities including golf course, leisure complex, Crown Green bowling, indoor heated swimming pool, award winning Murray's Restaurant and relaxing Bistro. Peace and tranquillity at affordable prices. Tel: 01624 661111 Fax: 01624 611116. See page 5

NARROWGATE HOUSE, Old Laxey Hill, Laxey, Isle of Man IM4 7DA. Home from home friendly run guest house overlooking Laxey Bay and harbour, 2 mins from beach. Two double rooms with colour TV, tea/coffee making facilities, hair dryers and radio. TV lounge also available. Tel: 01624 861966

NOBLES PARK Temporary campsite available TT fortnight; flush toilets, H&C water, showers, electricity. Otherwise campsite at Grandstand, Douglas with full facilities (Camping ~ no caravans) Tel: 01624 621132. See Page 43

NORTHWICH HOLIDAY APARTMENTS, 7 Mona Terr, Ideal central situation overlooking the wide sweep of Douglas Bay with commanding views. Quiet location write or phone for further details. Tel 01624 823752. See page 37.

SEFTON HOTEL, The Island's best loved hotel perfectly situated and packed with a whole range of facilities. Popular all year round, it is an ideal base to explore the Island from. Good food in Bistro/Restaurant, Cofee Shop. Tel: 01624 626011. See page 28

STAKIS HOTEL • CASINO, Central Promenade, Douglas IM2 4NA. Centrally located for tourists and the finance centre. Facilities include health club with pool, saunas, steam rooms and gymnasium, nightclub and casino. Concessionary green fees available for the championship course at Castletown. Tel: 01624 662662. Fax: 01624 625535. See page 36

STONELEIGH HOTEL, 20 Loch Promenade, Douglas. The Stoneleigh is probably the best value hotel in Douglas. Everything you need for the enjoyment of your stay on the Island. Spotlessly clean, comfortable and close to all amenities. Please telephone for further details. Tel: 01624 626125.See page 35

"THE SEAFIELD", 14 Empire Terrace, Douglas, Isle of Man. Superb licenced guest house. Overlooking the sea. Central for all entertainments. **B&B £12.00.** Child reductions. Large groups especially welcomed. Licenced bar. Tea/coffee, ironing facilities. Ample parking. Emphasis on comfort & friendliness. Fully inclusive travel/accommodation arranged. Tel: 01624 674372

SELF CATERING FLAT, 29 Laurel Avenue, Birchill, Onchan. Sleeping up to four. £10 per head per night (£12 during TT fortnight). Available throughout the year. Close to Douglas, yet country aspect, large secluded garden, off road parking, near bus route. Tel: 01624 673003

REGAL HOTEL, Queens Promenade, Douglas. 20 yards from beach and 100 yards from casino, in centre of Douglas Promenade. This hotel has been owned and operated by the Turner family since 1974. Special offers for over 55s are shown in our free colour brochure, available upon request. Tel: 01624 622876 Fax: 01624 624402. See page 32

"VERONA", 10 and 13, Stanley Terrace, Broadway, Douglas. Welcome to Verona self-contained holiday flats Douglas. Perfectly situated near beach and Villa Marina. Either ground, first, or second floor - none higher. All have double glazing for your warmth and comfort - plus large gardens. Tel: 01624 851603

THE WELBECK HOTEL, Mona Drive, off Central Promenade. Private family run hotel offering comfortable accommodation. Fresh food cooked by excellent chefs. Homely and friendly atmosphere. Tel: 01624 675663. See Page 34

PEEL & THE WEST

BALLAGAWNE COTTAGE, Glen Mooar, Kirk Michael, I.O.M. Ideally situated, this delightfully renovated eighteenth century stone cottage, full of character, has two bedrooms, family room etc. All mod cons, well furnished, large lawned garden, and stream. 150 yards to quiet beach. Brochure available. Tel/Fax: Geoff Dixon 01624 878429

COACH HOUSE COTTAGES, The Coach House, Ballaterson Beg, Ballaugh, Isle of Man IM7 5BN. Two comfortable detached one-bedroomed cottages with small enclosed gardens within owners grounds in delightfully peaceful country setting. Approx. 1.5 miles from shop and shore. Sleep up to four. Regret no smokers or pets. Tel: 01624 898026

FERNLEIGH PRIVATE HOTEL, Marine Parade, Peel, Isle of Man IM5 1PB. Our small hotel is in an excellent position for everything in Peel or rest of the Island. Very popular accommodation, early booking essential, mid week, early or late months. All welcome, excellent reputation. Travel arranged. Tel: 01624 842435

THE HAVEN, 10 Peveril Avenue, Peel IM5 1QB. Homely guest house, non-smoking, superior en-suite accommodation, CTV tea/coffee facilities, central heating. Open all year, lovely views, parking, evening meals. B&B from £16 pp. 3 Crowns Highly Commended. Phone Anthea for accommodation Air/Sea package. Travel services ATOL 1965 ABTA 7496. Tel: 01624 842585

HOLIDAY COTTAGE, 4 Charles Street, Peel, Isle of Man. Beautifully furnished 1700's fisherman's sandstone cottage for 2-3. In conservation area. Two bedrooms. Near harbour, beach and shops. Available all year. Highly Commended by Tourist Board. Contact:- Mrs Frost, Brack-A-Broom, Peel IM5 2AP. Tel: 01624 842270

'KIOWE TURRYS', 23 Douglas Street, Peel, Isle of Man. Attractively furnished 'homely' cottage ideally situated in the heart of Peel. By coastal footpath, golf course and all facilities. Fully equipped plus extras. Quality assured. Sleeps 4. Elec., towels & linen included. Car parking. Low season flexible. Tel: 01624 842233

"ROSEBANK", Tynwald Road, Peel, Isle of Man IM5 1JN. Five keys highly commended bungalow in pleasant surroundings adjoining owners home. 5 minutes walk to shops, beach, golf course.

On bus route. Linen and electricity provided. Private Parking. No pets. Tel: 01624 842600

SEAFORTH HOUSE, Crown Street, Peel. Lovely Manx guesthouse in sun set city. Adjacent to harbour and close to beach, shops, restaurant, pubs and facilities. Good base for exploring castle, cliff walks. Write or phone Mrs Plumley for further details. Tel: 01624 843404

STANSFIELD, Main Road, Dalby, Nr Peel. Quality studio apartment (detached), Dalby. New and fully equipped for two. Magnificent uninterrupted sea views over Irish Sea, lounge, fitted kitchen shower room, one bedroom (double bed), balcony. 3 Keys Commended. Fully inclusive price £250 per week. Open 12 months. Contact Mrs Talbot, Tel: 01624 842959

WALDICK HOTEL, Promenade, Peel, Isle of Man. Come to John and Maureen and our friendly staff. The only residential licenced house in Peel. Situated on sea front overlooking castle, and adjacent to bowling green and tennis courts. Please write or phone for our colour brochure. Tel: 01624 842410

WEST VIEW, Dalby, Peel, Isle of Man IM5 3BR. Cosy country cottage with garden. Sea and country views. Ideal walking, fishing, birdwatching area. Fully furnished, sleeps 4. Short distance away: golf, swimming, windsurfing, canoeing, boating, pony trekking, coach tours. Sorry no pets. Tel: 01624 842716

WESTVIEW COTTAGE, 3 Chapel Row, Higher Foxdale, I.O.M. IM4 3EF. Beautifully appointed self-contained manx croft set in Westview Cottage grounds. Teletext TV, courtesy tray, clock/radio. Close to pub, shop, garage. Breakfast served in our own beamed kitchen. One Crown Commended. Non smoking only. Tel.01624 801501

RAMSEY & THE NORTH

HILLSIDE, Ballaghennie, Bride. Detached Manx stone house situated in lovely countryside with extensive sea views. Own gardens, garage and parking. Clean spacious and well equipped home from home, sleeps 7, 4 bedrooms. 4 Keys. Come and enjoy a happy relaxing holiday. Contact: Mrs Desmond, 33 Rheast Mooar Lane, Ramsey. Tel: 01624 812303 or 880334

KERROWMOAR HOUSE, Sulby, Lezayre, Ramsey IM7 2AX. Charming Georgian country house north of Island offering deluxe accommodation, gardens, swimming pool, home-baked everything. Tel: 01624 897543, Fax: 01624 897927. See page 83

THE LIGHTHOUSE, Point of Ayre IM7 4BS. Fully furnished well equipped apartment located within the private grounds of a working lighthouse. Ideal for walking, ornithology, coastal fishing or just pure relaxation. Sleeps five in comfort. £150 - £250 per week. Tel: 01624 880832 Fax: 01624 880273

RECTORY COTTAGE, Kirk Andreas, Ramsey. Tastefully renovated Victorian cottage in village. Fully equipped for four people in two bedrooms. Gas, c/heating, electric, linen included. Modern bathroom, fitted kitchen, large lounge, separate sitting room. Regret no pets. Full details on application. Tel: 01624 880396

STEPPING STONE COTTAGE, Ramsey. Convenient cottage quietly situated in Ramsey. Sleeps three (two bedrooms). Central heating, TV, telephone, laundry. 4 Keys award. Approximately £129 to £189 pw plus power (1996). No pets, toddlers. Long winter lets from £69 (unserviced). Tel: 01624 880433

SUNNY RAMSEY. Self catering in superior accommodation. Fully equipped (4-5 Key). Family house/flats. Facilities for most disabled guests. Short/long term rental all year. Relief carer or maid on request. Contact Scopeland Ltd. Tel: 01624 812729/815956. See page 83

SUNNYSIDE COTTAGE, Ballajora, Maughold, Isle of Man IM7 1AZ. Charming old Manx cottage in lovely rural area; three miles from Ramsey, half mile from sea. Well equipped and comfortable. Off road parking, garden and views. Four star grading. Tel: 01624 812545

PORT ST MARY & THE SOUTH

BALLADUKE FARMHOUSE, Ballabeg, Arbory, Isle of Man IM9 4HD. Luxury self catering family accommodation situated on small working farm, enjoying sea and country views. 4 bedrooms sleeps 6 comfortably. All linen provided, cot available, No meters or hidden extras. 4 Keys Highly Commended. Tel: 01624 822250

BAY VIEW HOTEL, Bay View Road, Port St Mary, Isle of Man IM9 5AP. Family run hotel with licensed bars and private car park, good pub-grub and beer garden. Most rooms en-suite with TV and tea/coffee making facilities. Resident pianist plays each evening. Real ales. Children welcome. Tel: 01624 832234

BEACH CROFT GUEST HOUSE, Beach Road, Port St Mary, Isle of Man. Tastefully appointed family run guest house ensuring you of quality personal service. First class breakfast with choice of menu. Situated near*bus, train, shops, pubs and restaurants. Beautiful coastal scenery. Your home away from home. Tel: 01624 834521

CHERRY TREE HOUSE, Creggan Lea, Port St Mary, I.O.M. Cherry Tree House recently built luxury house on outskirts of village, 3 bedrooms extra downstairs loo, furnished to very high standard, lovely quiet country views. No hidden extras. For brochure Tel: 834932/833502

FISTARD COTTAGE, Fistard, Port St Mary, Isle of Man. Non smoking holiday home, sleeps 4, self catering, fully equipped. Regret no young children or pets. Near golf course. Tourist Board approved 3 Keys. Tel: 833557

HOLIDAY HOUSE, 7 The Quay, Port St Mary, Isle of Man. Superb panoramic view across quiet harbour to hills. Tastefully furnished fully-equipped home for 2-4. Three en-suite bedrooms, one with shower. Garage. Available all year. Highly Commended by Tourist Board. Contact:- Mrs Frost, Brack-A-Broom, Peel IM5 2AP. Tel: 01624 842270

THE POINT APARTHOTEL, Port St Mary, Isle of Man. Self-contained holiday apartments, fully equipped and furnished to a high standard. Unrivalled position near to breakwater - sea and coastal views. Adjacent to golf course and tennis courts. Two well furnished bars in complex. Contact Mr and Mrs McCutcheon for brochure. Tel: 01624 833238/833366

RONAGUE HOLIDAY HOMES, Ballafodda Farm, Ballabeg. Countryside chapel and farmhouse, four miles from Port Erin and Airport. Garden, spectacular views, children and dogs welcome. Tel: 01624 823355 See page 55

PORT ERIN & THE SOUTH

"AALIN", SEA FRONT HOLIDAY FLATS, Promenade, Port Erin, Isle of Man IM9 6LE. Premier position overlooking Bay. Beach, shops, car park, golf, nearby. Every flat (except one) has two bedrooms, lounge/kitchen, bathroom, toilet. Bed linen included. Midweek bookings. No pets. From £79 to £239 per flat per week. Three Keys Approved. Tel: 01624 835220

COLDEN COTTAGES. Three comfortable cottages, one a pretty bungalow in Port Erin with private garden, suitable for the elderly. Two attractive cottages in Bradda (one Manx) with magnificent views over golf course and Port Erin and Fleshwick Bays. Enquiries to:- Cronkbane House, Oak Hill, Braddan, Isle of Man IM4 1AR. Tel: 01624 623286

FALCON'S NEST HOTEL, Port Erin. Victorian elegance and the natural beauty of Port Erin await you at the Falcon's Nest. Tel: 01624 834077 Fax: 01624 835370. See page 64

GROSVENOR HOTEL, The Promenade, Port Erin, Isle of Man. Warm, clean, friendly hotel where you can count on care, comfort, courtesy and excellent cuisine. All rooms with colour TVs, tea-makers, radio and baby listening. Licensed bar and games rooms. En-suites available. From £15 B&B. Tel: 01624 834124

PORT ERIN HOTELS LTD, A selection of four quality hotels from 2 Crown to 4 Crown, fully en suite. Nightly entertainment. Competitive package prices available. Caters for a wide range of clientele with extensive menu choice and friendly experienced staff. Telephone for colour brochure. Tel: 01624 833116. See page 62

REGENT HOUSE, Promenade, Port Erin, Isle of Man. Small friendly guest house. TV, tea making, clock/radio in all bedrooms. Choice of vegetarian and standard menus. Central heating. Six twin/double en-suite rooms. Sorry no smokers or small children. Simply the best. Tel:(01624) 833454. See Page 63

CASTLETOWN

ROPEWALK, c/o Ballamoar, Douglas Road, Castletown. Sea-front large detached house. Sleeps 9. 5 Keys. Also, attractive cottage and apartment. Situated in the ancient capital of Man, with its centuries old castle and picturesque harbour. Convenient to bus and steam trains. Great base for exploring island. Tel: 01624 823830

THE ROWANS, Douglas Street, Castletown. Peaceful situation overlooking bay. Castle, nautical museum, heritage and shops all close by. Easy access to rest of island by car, bus or steam train. Friendly personal service by proprietor Mrs F M Jelly. Dinner provided on request. Tel: 01624 823210

Index

Discount Voucher

Acknowledgements

The Publishers would like to thank the Honourable Tony Brown MHK, Minister of the Isle of Man Department of Tourism, Leisure and Transport, for writing the foreword to this publication. Our thanks also go to Terry Toohey and David Barrow, of the Isle of Man Department of Tourism, Leisure and Transport for their support and valuable assistance. The Publishers would also like to thank the following for their assistance:Doreen Douglas (Celt Marketing and Research), Mike Bates, Annie Lowey, Pat Somner and Julie Towler (Lily Publications (IOM) Ltd.), and all our Advertisers for their generosity.